SHE CAN

SHE CAN

31 Day Devotional

Becoming the woman you were created to be while walking into your destiny

NAJMA CALHOUN

Dedication

The She Can 31-Day Devotional is dedicated to:

My father, Daddy, thank you for always depositing wisdom inside of me. I'm better because of you. I'm better because of your unconditional love. I'm better because of the ways you push me beyond my limits. I love you so much.

My mother, Mommy, thank you for bringing me into this world. I am here because of you. Thank you for teaching me how to operate in different capacities. The skills you showed me, the ideas you've birthed inside of me, and the love you've always had for me are things I can't imagine life without. I love you so much.

My brother, Sardaar, you are my inspiration and my motivation. I never thought that having a little brother would have an impact on me the way it does but you've left an imprint on my heart that no man can ever take away from me. The love I have for you is indescribable. Thank you for always motivating me to be my best and work hard no matter what. I love you, Khadir.

To all my sisters and friends that were encouraging me during my writing process. Your encouragement and prayers helped me finish my first book. For every phone call I had to reschedule, every brunch missed, and every trip I had to postpone. I thank you so much for your grace and love. I will forever be by your side. I love you.

Table of Contents

Introduction 1

Day 1: Circling Back 5

Day 2: Reimaging Yourself From the Inside Out 10

Day 3: Rekindling Your Relationship with God 14

Day 4: Faith Levels 20

Day 5: The Power of Prayer 24

Day 6: Mind Dumping 33

Day 7: Running on Empty 38

Day 8: Hustle Culture 43

Day 9: Gut Check 47

Day 10: Keep It Moving 54

Day 11: Is Therapy for Me? 58

Day 12: Sister! Sister! 65

Day 13: Bad Breath 70

Day 14: Unrooting Comparison 74

Day 15: Soul Maintenance 78

Day 16: Resetting Love 81

Day 17: Parental Trauma 85

Day 18: Mother Nature 90

Day 19: Activating Spiritual Gifts 95

Day 20: Financial Discernment 100

Day 21: Doubt or Destiny 104

Day 22: Confront Your Distractions 108

Day 23: Social Mess 113

Day 24: Bible Intimidation 119

Day 25: Welcome Aboard 125

Day 26: Trust the Transition 131

Day 27: The Power of Your Yes 137

Day 28: Obedience Over Perfection 142

Day 29: Clarity Over Courage 148

Day 30: Overlooked 151

Day 31: She Can - She Is You 155

About the Book 158

Introduction

Hi Sister,

There has probably been a time in your life when you have asked this wavering question. Can I really change? Can I live out the dreams that are planted in my heart? Can I heal from the things that have brought me so much grief and pain? Or will it all remain the same?

Perhaps this question creeps into your mind once a week, once a month, or a few times a year. The question, "Can I change?" is rooted in a place of fear and uncertainty. Uncertainty about your life and future. God looks at your uncertainty like His responsibility. He sees how eager you are to experience transformation. You can't see the totality of who God created you to be, but God sees it very clearly, each and every day. The trials that you have gone through do not mess up God's plan for your life. The trials are just stepping stones, setting you up for what's ahead. You'll understand why you went through the things you went through, in due time.

Sister, I wonder if you think you can't change because you're focused on your past, your age, your fears, and your pain. Well, sister, I am here to tell you that you can change! You already are changing! This is the first step to moving toward a better version of yourself! Keep taking small steps forward and watch how God will do the rest!

Can I tell you something else? When this book entered your hands, we became sisters. As you go through the book, day by day, imagine we are together having brunch, in our pajamas, or out for a friendly walk. I'm so excited to spend the next 31 days with you. God's excited too. Get ready to feel and experience transformation.

Over the next 31 days, you are going to gain clarity from God in areas that appear blurry. You're going to gain access to heaven's resources that have always been waiting for you. You're going to get to know yourself in a more vulnerable way. The areas that you had closed off from God, you're about to open them back up. Then healing, dreaming, and evolving will begin.

Each of these daily devotions has been prayed over, specifically for you. Each daily devotion also has a "Soul Food and Soul Work" section. Let me explain!

Soul Food Section: Who doesn't love good food? The Soul Food Section is where you digest good nourishment for your soul. This section should make your body, mind, and spirit happy and excited every time you receive it. This will include Bible verses, quotes, prayers, declarations, and mindset tools. It isn't designed to be a temporary taste but rather a long-term impression.

Soul Work Section: You experience peace when your soul feels healthy. The Soul Work Section is when you activate your faith and do what's necessary to have a healthy mind, spirit, and soul. This will include affirmations, challenges, journal prompts, and growth tools. The Soul Work Section is designed to show you all you're capable of. Discipline and consistency will be produced when you implement your soul work.

Are you ready sister? You're about to meet a version of yourself that you've never met before. You're not going to be able to recognize her. Your life is about to drastically change because your mindset is about to change. You can get your joy back. You can release fears and finally stand on faith. You can let depression go and welcome peace. You're about to get more intimate with God and get connected to the right people. God is about to give you a new lens to see a glimpse of all He has for you. You've been hiding for far too long. It's time to rise up and be the woman you were called to be even when it's not easy. There are assignments only you can complete. There's territory that you only have access to. I know the devil has been telling you that you can't do it, but God's saying SHE will do it.

She is coming out. She's coming back. She's ready. God's saying, "I got her and she's got me".

Go ahead and exhale the word "can't" and inhale the word "can." Because you can and will be the woman you were destined to be.

I'm so excited to see what God is about to do in your life. Thank you for letting me walk alongside you on this journey.

She Can - She Is You

Love your sister,

Najma Calhoun

DAY 1:

Circling Back

She Can circle back to the place she once avoided but she won't park there.

Have you ever heard the saying, "Your past is your past, leave it there" or "Forget what happened to you, and move forward"? I used to operate and live my life by both of those sayings. Every time I remembered a glimpse of my past, I would try to escape it as quickly as possible. I would run away from the thought, so fast, as if I was running away from a vicious dog, chasing me down a road. I kept running because I wasn't ready to face what happened. So I would dodge every thought, every conversation, and every flashback that reminded me of my past.

Running and hiding caused me to become numb to what happened to me. There were days when my feelings felt locked and my heart felt caved. On the days I didn't have the words, my tears did the talking. On the days when my past made me angry, my actions expressed my outrage. And ultimately these actions embarrassed me to my core because I knew the root of it was my pain.

Getting pregnant and having an abortion as a teenage girl is a feeling that I can't fully explain. I just remember asking myself, "How did I get here?"

Sister, have you ever asked yourself: How did I get here? Why did I do that? What brought me to this point? If you are anything like me, those questions haunted me for years. My thoughts always answered with guilt, shame, embarrassment, and a lot of condemnation. Escaping my past became my new normal.

I realized I couldn't run anymore. I had cried my last tear. My poor lungs couldn't take anymore from running. It was just me, God, and my past facing each other all at once. We were confronting the elephant in the room. I stood in the most uncomfortable and vulnerable position. But even in the uncomfortableness, I felt peace. That peace was God's presence inviting me to **circle back,** to circle back to the root of my pain and my past.

I disagree with many statements that encourage us to avoid our past, forget our past, and run from our past, because it's almost impossible to forget and avoid the pain you experience that you never got a chance to process. Now sister, don't get me wrong, I don't believe that we should live in the past. Our past is not a place where we should park, but it is a place to circle back and revisit. How can we walk freely in our present and our future if we don't acknowledge our past?

So today, I want us to get back in the car and circle back, to some of the things in our past. Before we start let's take a deep breath in and then breathe out. Repeat that 3 times. I want to give you a heads-up that we aren't going to park here long but we are going to park while we process. We have to take time to process the dream we gave up on, the unforgiveness we are holding on to, the divorce, the miscarriage, the rape, and the molestation experienced at a young age. Each of these experiences brought us pain that we have to take time to heal through.

See sister, our past doesn't have to mess us up, but can be used by God to set up our futures. Some days you might ask why you went through the things you went through. There are probably days where you ask yourself: Why me? I didn't deserve this. We may never get an answer. But what if our past could bring us closer to God? What if there is another sister that is about to come into your path that God needs you to minister to? Perhaps only you can minister to her because you have been down that road before. What if your past can be used for something bigger than you?

Sister, we have been down, long enough, hiding from our past, dodging our past, embarrassed by our past. It's time for us to come out and circle back. It might be painful, it might be uncomfortable, but where God is taking us, He needs us to acknowledge the pieces we have ignored. You are not defined by your past. Your past is not your birth certificate. Your past is not the definition of who you are.

If we were in church right now I hope you would be shouting "YESSSSSS" from the front row, maybe the choir, in the lobby, or virtually.

Maybe our past has been holding us hostage. It's been stopping us from doing the things God has called us to. Perhaps we have parked in our past, we may even be living in our past, rather than just taking a moment and processing. Our stories can help us grow, motivate others, draw closer to God, grow in wisdom, and mature in different areas.

Our past wasn't meant to take control over our life. Today we will no longer try to escape our past but we will embrace it, including both the broken pieces and the beautiful pieces. Let's look at our past like a passport, all the beautiful places it can take us, only if we believe.

Soul Food:

As we are circling back, let's do exactly what **Psalm 37:5 (GNT)** says. "Give yourself to the LORD; trust in Him, and He will help you". In order for these next 31 days to be the most impactful days of our life we need God's help as we are circling back into uncomfortable territory. What territory in your life do you need to confront?

Soul Work:

Today, write about the feeling, situation, or the past experience that you have often avoided. Write how it made you feel, or any frustrations you have by it, or maybe how it has caused you to stay stuck. End the journal prompt by asking God to help you as you begin to circle back and process your past. Take it easy as you are writing, sister. Be gentle with yourself.

DAY 2:

Reimaging Yourself From the Inside Out

She held her head up high because she knew a new version of herself was approaching.

Sister, can I ask you a question. When people ask who you are, how do you answer them? Typically, as women, we define ourselves by our job, by our kids, maybe by how much money we make, or by our family. Do you realize that you are more than your job, children, salary, career, relationship status, or your body?

Sister, there is so much more to you than a title. What made you lose sight of who you are? What made you start believing less about yourself?

I think I might have a clue why you stopped focusing and believing in yourself. Maybe it's because we have been focusing on and believing what the devil and people say about us instead of what God says about us. If you agree with me: just say, "Yes Sis!"

Those negative thoughts have to stop, sister. Do an exercise with me for the next few minutes. Start with bringing your body to a relaxing and still point. Now, take a moment to be vulnerable. I want you to go to the place that makes you feel most uncomfortable about yourself. Go to that insecurity that you always try to hide. Go to the deepest fear that you have. Stay there for a few moments. Even if it feels uncomfortable. What thoughts come to your mind while you are there? Don't rush this process. A lot of times we try to dismiss what's going on inside of us but today we are bringing attention to it. After you are finished looking, I want you to pray. Pray for yourself. Pray for your healing. Pray for the way you imagine and view yourself. Pray for God's help and guidance.

Take it one step at a time. Reimagining yourself isn't easy especially if you've been bruised, lied to, or if you've been failed. Sister, I know you've been through a lot. I bet most days you are just trying to figure out "who I am". Keep discovering who you are. I believe that's where God is trying to take you to the next level of who you are. The vision that you have about yourself, right now, isn't the same vision that God has about you. If God believes in you, then you have to start believing in yourself too.

Sister, we have to confront some of the things that the devil has been lying to you about. I'll start with this: no man or no relationship is going to define who you are anymore. What God has for you is not based on your relationship status. The false self-image that you have is not going to define who you are anymore or where you are going. Your children are not going to define the woman you are capable of being. You are more than a mother. Your past is not going to define the places God is about to take you. In fact, your past qualifies you for the places that you are about to enter. Do I need to go any further? I tried to make it as plain as I could, but I'm tired of the devil and I'm tired of the lies he has convinced you to believe about yourself.

You are God's daughter. Yes, you have been shattered in different areas but you are going to experience healing. You are beautiful no matter your size, the color of your skin, or your hair texture. It is time to start reimagining yourself as the millionaire you want to be. It is time to start reimagining yourself as a healthy woman. Start imagining yourself doing the things that bring you joy and the things you have always dreamed of. Ephesians 3:20 helps us understand the importance of us imagining and believing bigger than what our eyes can naturally see. "Now to him who is able to do immeasurably more than all we ask or imagine, according to His power that is at work within us" (NIV).

Start doing things that actually make you happy instead of trying to make everyone else happy. Yes, I said it - and if they have a problem with it, send them my way because you are shifting your focus and reimagining the woman God created you to be.

We are sisters, and we are going to stand together. So I will leave you with this. **She is ready to come out. She is not gone. Go and find her. She is you.**

Soul Food:

"Anyone who belongs to Christ is a new person. The past is forgotten, and everything is new" **2 Corinthians 5:17 (CEV).**

Soul Work:

Take a moment and research what your name means. Then write your own unique meaning of what your name means to you. After you are done, write a letter to yourself, talking to yourself gently. Share about who you are and who you are becoming. Then make a promise to yourself to refocus on yourself again.

DAY 3:

Rekindling Your Relationship with God

She is ready to reconnect with her creator.

Sister, I want to ask you a very personal question. How is your current relationship with God? Do you feel like it has been hard to connect with God because of a situation that happened to you? Do you feel like you are hiding from God because of something you did that you are ashamed of? Maybe your relationship with God is pretty good, but you're just trying to make it a more consistent relationship. Or are you trying to figure out what your relationship status is?

No matter where you are, you can rekindle your relationship with God. No matter what you have done, you can rekindle your relationship with God. You may not know the reason for a particular situation or thing which happened to you, but you can talk with God about it. I've been reading the book of Exodus and I am learning about Moses. Sister, read Exodus 2-3, when you get a chance. Can we call Moses our big brother? He really is a brother in Christ and humanity.

I'm not going to give away the whole story but Moses ends up killing someone. After he kills the person he hides their body in the sand, and he thinks no one will ever find out what he has done. You are probably saying, "Moses is not our brother". Hold on sis, it gets juicy. So the Egyptians and Pharaoh find out that Moses has killed an Egyptian and now they want to kill Moses. But before they can kill him, Moses runs far, far away, and hides.

Long story short, Moses hides from the people that want to kill him. He then hides from his family and God because he is so ashamed of what he has done. Moses goes into the wilderness for some quiet time and God speaks to Him. God wants to talk to Moses about how He wants to use him. God wants to tell Moses how He wants to make him a great leader. But Moses, in that moment, hides from God.

The reason I say Moses is our brother is because we often hide from God after we have done something we are ashamed of. Moses is like us, sister. We have done some things that we aren't so proud of. We knew better, but we didn't do better. That is because we aren't perfect. We are humans that will make mistakes. In the midst of our guilt and shame, we have lost sight of our relationship with God. Thoughts run through our heads that God may be upset with us. Those thoughts replay and then turn into "God doesn't love me" or "God isn't with me anymore". Our mistakes aren't meant to disconnect us from God, they are supposed to bring us closer to God.

It blows my mind how God and Moses reconnected in Exodus 3. Usually, when a child does something wrong, parents want to discuss what happened, so they can avoid doing it again. Watch this, when God and Moses reconnect God doesn't even bring up what Moses did years ago when he killed the Egyptian. Instead, God talked with Moses about how He needs Moses to lead His people. Say what! God wanted a murderer to lead His people? See, our mistakes just invite us into God's mercy and grace.

God sees past the things we examine every day. I wonder if the story of Moses goes for us as well sister? God isn't focused on our mistakes or what we did in the past, He just wants us to reconnect with Him. He just wants us to fulfill the purpose and plan He has over our life. He wants us to use the gifts He birthed us with. God is not upset with you. If God wants to rekindle His relationship with Moses, a man who killed someone then I know He wants to rekindle His relationship with you.

The word rekindle means - "relight". Sister, that means it's time to relight your relationship with God. It's time to stop hiding from God and come in God's presence. You need God and God wants you. Why wouldn't you want to rekindle your relationship with the person that created you and knew you, before your mother knew you? God is the person that knows everything about your now and your future. Isn't it crazy how we try to rekindle relationships with people that have no purpose for our lives, but when was the last time we tried to rekindle our relationship with God?

    Sister, it's time. You might not have talked to God in a while, but it's time to start communicating with Him again. You might only pray when something goes wrong, but it's time to pray during the good and the bad. You might be ashamed of what you did, but it's time to forgive yourself. You might have lost trust in God, but it's time to rebuild your trust in Him. Whatever has been going on in your life, it's time to include God in the mix. Sister, I can relate to Moses on so many levels because when I had an abortion as a teenage girl, I hid from God. I also hid from myself during that season because I had so much guilt and shame. I then became numb to my pain. I'm not sure if you have ever been in that boat before, but I've included 3 tips to help us rekindle our relationship with God.

> » **Tip 1: Presenting Our Mess:** I think as women we have been taught to present ourselves in such a "put together" way, all the time. We often translate that same idea when we have to present ourselves to God. Listen, God accepts all of our mess. He wants us to come just as we are. Try going to God with your mess. Try going to God without saying the perfect prayer. Try singing the worship song even if you don't know all the words, just let the spirit move you. Here's an announcement for all the "church folk": you don't have to know all the Bible Verses in the Bible to have

a relationship with God. Just present yourself to God just the way you are. He can handle all of you.

- **Tip 2: Confronting The Hard Stuff:** Having hard conversations is hard. There isn't a way we can move past that. However, it's better to say something rather than nothing at all. As you are rekindling your relationship with God, confront the hard stuff. Express to God how you have been feeling. Confront the things you have been feeling towards God. God is an open God and He's always ready to listen. You will be amazed at how God comforts you when you express the hard stuff.

- **Tip 3: Learn God's Love Language:** In any relationship you have to spend quality time with one another to get to know each other. Find time in your schedule each day to spend time with God. It could be 5 mins, 10 mins, or 15 mins. Just spend time with God. You will learn more about Him and you will become closer to Him each and every day.

How can you spend time with him? Listen to encouraging sermons, talks, or Podcasts about God or an area you want to improve in your life. Order a study Bible in a version which you understand and resonate with. "YouTube University" is our friend, sister, and we can find tools there as well. Incorporate more worship music into your daily schedule. Journal to God. Go on walks with God. Incorporate moments where you simply pray and then listen to what God has to say. You and God will grow closer. This will also help you understand God's love language.

Soul Food:

"I am the God who was worshiped by your ancestors Abraham, Isaac, and Jacob." Moses was afraid to look at God, and so He hid his face." ***Exodus 3:6 (CEV)***

Soul Work:

Take your journal out, sister. If you have a Bible, take that out as well. If you don't have one, that's no problem, there are so many different Bible apps and Bible websites you can access. Take a moment to read Exodus chapters 2 and 3. They are very short chapters. And then, write down three lessons you learned from those chapters. Also, include what stood out to you about Moses' story and his conversation with God on the mountain. My hope is that you see the proof of how much God loves you and how God doesn't use your past against you. God doesn't block any blessings from you because of things you have done in your past. You have full access to Him and everything that He has in store for you.

Day 4:

Faith Levels

She learns that faith cannot fully activate until she gets into a position of trust.

Sister, for some time I believed that the words "faith and trust" were the same. But I was wrong. They are very similar words, but have very different meanings and actions connected to them.

When we have faith we are hopeful and expectant for the impossible to take place. (see Hebrews 11:1) We are believing in something we can't physically see. When we have faith our eyes shift and see things from a more positive perspective with endless possibilities connected. Faith is when you have no idea how you will afford one of your bills, but you are hopeful that somehow it will be paid anyways.

Trust is an act of surrender. When you trust, you get into a position of total reliance. Trust is taking a situation out of your hands and placing it into another's. A form of trust is when you leave your child with someone that you hope will take good care of them until you return. You trust their character, you trust their reliability. You have placed your child in their hands. You have formed a level of trust with them because they have shown themselves as trustworthy. This is when you are operating in trust.

Sister, I want to ask you this. Do you operate more in faith or more in trust? Would you say that you operate in them both? If you have faith and trust, then why do you keep worrying the way you do? I'm not saying that worry will never come, but if you trust God with your situation then you have taken things out of your control and put everything in God's control. If you're realizing that you need to have more trust in God, that's okay, it is something that we all need to work on. Our relationship with God will mature even more when we fully surrender and trust Him.

There is nothing like being in a relationship, but one of the persons is hesitant to trust the other. They hesitate to fully be open and honest. They hesitate to be themselves, or to communicate vulnerably when things are going right and when things are going wrong.

The good thing is that God remains consistent. He remains reliable. He remains trustworthy. He remains loving. He remains loyal. God isn't someone we need to question if we can trust Him or not. God is someone to which we can surrender our load. We can trust that everything that concerns us will be taken care of when it is placed in God's hands.

Sister, keep having faith. Keep being hopeful and optimistic. God loves that! Now allow faith and trust to join together so you and God can grow to new levels together.

Soul Food:

Meditate on this scripture and let the words speak to you: "God is my savior; I will trust him and not be afraid. The LORD gives me power and strength; He is my Savior." ***Isaiah 12:2 (GNT).***

Soul Work:

Sister, here are six declarations to boldly recite and keep with you every day. Feel free to add more to this list. This is just the beginning of you declaring what God has for you. Three of the declarations are geared towards faith and the other three are geared towards trust.

- » I am hopeful that all things are working strategically for my good, by God.
- » I believe the best outcome is going to happen for my situation.
- » I will remain positive and optimistic when life throws me the unexpected.

- » I will put my total reliance on God, the one who has never steered me wrong.
- » I will trust in God because He has shown Himself to be consistent towards me.
- » I will take things out of my hands and place them into God's hands because they belong there.

DAY 5:

The Power of Prayer

> *She prays because it gives her access to things heaven already had in store for her.*

Sister, think about this with me. What if some of our prayers have never been answered because they have never been asked? This realization came to me during the "40-Day, Draw the Circle Prayer Challenge by Mark Batterson". Some of our hopes and desires in our lives haven't come to fruition because we haven't asked for the change we are desiring to see. I want to be clear. I learned the hard way, that prayer is not a tool to get what you want. God is not a magic wand; we can't wave the wand left and right to get what we are hoping for. Life has probably already taught us that prayer doesn't work that way.

God answers our prayers with either a yes, no, or not yet. The way God answers our prayers is in our best interest.

There are times we pray for something and the prayer is answered immediately. There was a time when I was almost homeless as I was headed into Graduate school. The housing opportunity that I thought I had, fell through. God answered my prayer quickly, as if He was saying "Baby girl, I need you to get that degree". You never know why God puts certain people on your path. Then one day you see all of the pieces to the puzzle begin to come together.

My parents-away-from-home in undergraduate school connected me with a wonderful family to live with while I would be in graduate school. This sweet couple took me in without hesitation. They had promised they would never house another person because of previous bad experiences, but God. God can soften an individual's heart just for you. I saw God do that clearly with this family that treated me as their own. Now I have adopted them as my aunt and uncle. God knew my needs before I knew my needs. God's orchestration isn't something we should doubt or question because He sees beyond what our eyes can see. I am so thankful that God blessed me with housing quickly. That's an example of when God answers a prayer, right away.

Then there are other times when God answers our prayers and says "no." I know we don't like to hear the word "no." I am learning that there is power in God's "no." God knows what's on the other side of what we are asking for. Like a job we pray for and God says no. God says no because He knows the people that work there. He knows their systems and how things operate. He knows what goes on behind the scenes. He knows there is disorganization within the company and He doesn't want to put us in that type of environment so He says "no."

God told me "no" when I wanted to join a missionary program where I would be able to travel the world for 11 months serving in 11 different countries. One month I would have been able to serve at an orphanage in Africa, then another month I would have been able to teach at a local school in India, then work in a health clinic in Thailand. Doesn't that sound amazing, sister? God said no almost immediately. Instead, I thought, "Why God? I'm going to serve your people". God's like "No sweet baby, I need you to serve in this different area for right now".

While I was asking God so many questions and debating His "no," He opened another opportunity for me to work with women that had been sex trafficked. This opportunity included a full-time job and free housing. In all of my complaining, frustration, and worry, God was looking at what was coming ahead. It wasn't until months later when I saw why God said no. A global pandemic came and the 11 month mission opportunity was shut down. Everything was canceled. The team was forced to return home because of the pandemic.

Imagine; I would have been trying to find a job and housing during the beginning of a pandemic. Instead, God knew what He was doing before the pandemic came. God was so strategic in those moments when He blessed me with a home and job. I remember feeling so unworthy when God presented those blessings, but God's grace was so heavy all I could do was thank Him. God revealed to me that serving women that had been sex trafficked was one of the best ways to serve in the world. Sometimes God's "no" is for our benefit. I didn't know the global pandemic was coming but God did. God's "no" was His way of protection over my life.

Then there are times when God answers and says "Not yet." I remember a few years ago I bought a promise ring for myself. I loved that ring. One day I ended up losing the ring and boy did I cry. I was so sad because of what the ring meant to me. I tore my house up looking for it. I called all of my family and friends that I had recently visited and asked them if they had seen it. The ring was nowhere to be found. It was about 2 years later that I found the ring under my dish mat. "God!

The place where I dry my dishes!" that's where the ring was for 2 years. I just laughed. I thought I would never find my ring again, but God. I wonder if God had to remove the ring because I was idolizing it in just the slightest way. I would have feelings of discomfort if I forgot to wear the ring. There were times when I didn't feel as connected with God if I wasn't wearing the ring. Since I dedicated the ring to myself and God. The message I believe God was trying to tell me was if you have the ring on or off that doesn't change my love for you. God was reiterating to me that we are always connected. A piece of jewelry does not determine how strong our connection is.

Sister, my point is to pray and never stop praying no matter what the answer may be. Don't put God on a timeline to answer your prayers because God knows the best time to answer your prayers. God sees things that we aren't able to see. That's why I say to ask, regardless of the answer you will receive. The word pray means "to make a request in a humble manner". Prayer means to "address God: which includes - confession, supplication, or thanksgiving".

Your prayers need to be recorded

Get a journal specifically for documenting your prayers. We will call this journal your prayer journal. You can keep track of all your prayer requests. Be specific and add a date and a time. When God answers a prayer, document it. Then go back and reflect on the things you prayed about and you will continue to see a continuation of God moving in your life. God is a God of surprises. Allow God to surprise you more often by you using the gift of prayer. Perhaps you are strengthening your prayer life or learning how to pray for the first time. Ask God for the words to say when you don't know what to pray about. He will help you. I wanted to provide some prayer tips that you can incorporate in your prayer life.

Prayer Tip #1: Beginning our prayers with Thanksgiving

A good way to start your prayers is to state what you are thankful for. We always have something to be thankful for! You can say, "Lord, I am thankful that you have woken me up to see another day!" You can share with God that you are thankful for your home, your family, and the job you don't have but hope is coming! What blessings have you seen in your life lately? Take time to thank God in prayer for them. Starting with a spirit of

Thanksgiving in prayer is always refreshing. Psalm 107:1 (NIV) says "Give thanks to the Lord, for He is good, His love endures forever". Let's incorporate this every time we pray.

Prayer Tip #2: Praying on behalf of others

Have you noticed that your family has been under attack recently? Instead of worrying and panicking about the situation, take it to God, in prayer. Take it out of your hands and place your family in God's hands. Sister, have you been having trouble with your children? Instead of saying "They are bad" or "It is impossible for them to change". Start going to God every single day on their behalf. Sometimes the words you have need to be used in prayer and not towards the person. Start praying for your co-workers, your friends, and people who mention that they need prayer. Sometimes, the best gift you can give a person is praying for them. Ephesians 6:18 (CEV) says, "Never stop praying, especially for others. Always pray by the power of the Spirit. Stay alert and keep praying for God's people".

Prayer Tip #3: Praying specifically for yourself

Sister, never feel selfish when you pray for yourself about direction for your life. Don't hold back anything. Communicate with God how you have been feeling. Express to God when things are starting to become unclear in your world. Just let the words flow out of your mouth. Sister, talk to God about your finances, your attitude, your job, and the business you want to start. Talk to God about anything that concerns your life.

A friend once told me, "I only talk to God about specific things, not everything." In my head, I said "oh noooo, honey, we don't serve the same God because the God I serve wants to know about any and everything happening in my life, because He cares". If you are single, ask God for wisdom and direction with the people you may date. If you are in a relationship or married, ask for God's guidance as you take the next steps. Talk to God about opening and closing doors for you. Sister, please don't forget to talk to God about all of your dreams and goals. Go to war during your prayer time. Ephesians 3:20 (CSB) says "Now to him who is able to do above and beyond all that we ask or think according to the power that works in us" Get ready for God to do the above and beyond in your life.

Where should I pray?

Sister, you might be wondering where a good place to pray is. I know this may sound dramatic but incorporate prayer everywhere. When I say everywhere, I mean everywhere. In the airport, at your job, at the restaurant, on vacation, in the hospital, in your home. In the morning when you wake up, start your day with prayer. When you enter your car, start praying for safety. Pray in your head. Journal your prayers. When folks start plucking the little bit of nerves you have left, say a prayer in your heart and mind for them and you. Make praying at night before bed a routine. Don't be ashamed to pray with people wherever you go.

Create a space for you and God:

Sister, it's time to create a special place in your home to have quiet and prayer time with God. This special place could be in your bedroom, closet, bathroom, kitchen, or living room.

You just need a place where you can run when you need God. Make this space special. Decorate this space and add things that inspire you. You might want to get a prayer rug. Be creative. Enjoy this new space. If your home doesn't allow for a space, then find a place outside your home where you can find peace and quiet time with yourself and God. It can be somewhere outdoors in nature, a coffee shop, or any sacred space. Just make sure there are limited distractions. Mathew 6:6 (GNT) says "But when you pray, go into your room, close the door, and pray to your Father, who is unseen. Then your Father, who sees what is done in secret will reward you".

A praying woman is a powerful woman and that woman is you. One of the things that is going to keep you grounded in this new season is your daily prayer life. Be intentional by not allowing anything to come in the way of your daily prayer time with God.

Soul Food:
1 Thessalonians 5:17
"Pray without ceasing" (ESV)
"Pray continually" (NIV)
"Pray without ceasing" (NKJV)
"Never stop praying" (NLT)
"Pray Constantly" (CSB)
"Pray at all times" (GNT)

Soul Work:

Here's a prayer challenge for you, sister. Pick a day that you will pray at three different times. Pray these three different prayers. Make each prayer five minutes. I suggest setting a timer if that will help.

- » Your first five-minute prayer will be your prayer of Thanksgiving and Praise. *Refer back to Prayer Tip #1.*
- » Your second five-minute prayer will be praying on behalf of others. *Refer back to Prayer Tip #2.*
- » Your third five-minute prayer will be praying specifically for yourself. *Refer back to Prayer Tip #3.*

DAY 6:

Mind Dumping

> *She will say every time the devil tells me that I can't do something I will remind him that I can do everything with God.*

    Sister, I can't help but correlate how our minds sometimes operate like storage on our phones. You know storage on a phone holds everything and it has so much space. It stores all of our apps, text messages, pictures, videos, and so much more. I don't like it when my phone alerts me with the message saying "Your storage is almost full". It's an annoying reminder because I don't like deleting things. I want to keep all the pictures, all the messages, and all the memories. I've noticed a lot of the things I'm storing and holding on to really should be deleted because it doesn't serve a purpose in my life anymore. Why do I need pictures of me and my ex-boyfriend on my phone? If I left that in the past why am I carrying it with me every day? Not everything that we store should remain in storage. Some things need to be discarded. Some things need to be dumped and go directly into the trash. I wonder if that's how we treat our minds. Storing things that should no longer be in our storage unit. Holding on to images that need to be dumped in the trash.

As soon as we make the choice to discard some thoughts, feelings, and wounds from out of our mind new storage becomes available to us. New space doesn't come unless something is taken out.

What are some things that you need to delete and dump from your mind, sister? What negative things are you believing about yourself? What comment did someone make about you that you can't get out of your head? What thoughts of guilt and shame do you let take hold of your mind each and every day? Can we take a moment to dump those things out? Your mind is no longer going to be the devil's playground. We are stopping that today.

As we are removing things out of storage there is now going to be space to fill new things. Now sister, you know when we have additional storage, we want to immediately fill the space. Be slow with adding new things (I'm still talking about your mind). Be selective. Not everything you think needs to be planted in your mind. Some thoughts need to be immediately released if it doesn't align with God.

Sister, sometimes you have to interrupt the devil right when he starts to plant lies in your mind. Interrupt him right when he tries to discourage you. Interrupt him when he tries to make you doubt yourself or your worth. In other words, cut the devil off. Stop the nonsense he is trying to begin in your mind. Remember we serve a powerful God. A God that can help us overcome any and everything. A God that is more powerful than some little devil that is trying to attack our minds.

Sometimes we are the one's taking up unjust storage in our minds, instead of the devil. Telling yourself that you can't do something, you won't do something, things will never get better. Break up with your cycle of thoughts that keep breaking you. God is taking you to where your current mindset can't go. God is taking you into something new so your mindset has to become new. Today we are breaking up with our negative thought pattern. We're dumping things. Let's get rid of the things that we stored for way too long. And then, let's focus on ways we can feed our mind positive things. Let's call this replacing storage.

3 WAYS TO FEED YOUR MIND:

1. Watch positive and encouraging material. It can be a motivational video, a sermon, or something that makes you laugh. Let's be honest, the news and social media can bring fear, comparison, or stress. Then those feelings turn into triggers then those triggers start to form negative thoughts in our mind. Let's start watching things that bring us peace, joy, and inspiration.

2. Listen to a positive song, a Podcast, soothing music, an audible book, or words of affirmation. The words that we listen to impact the thoughts that enter our minds. Let's start listening to positivity because we know the effects of listening to negativity. Can I get an "Amen," sister? Create a playlist and title it "the positive playlist".

3. Be still. I know being still is hard, sister. Our minds can race a thousand miles per hour with many thoughts and feelings. We have to take time to allow our minds to slow down and rest. When your mind starts racing, practice journaling, meditating, and praying. Make time to rest or go for a walk.

Repeat this statement: "My mind is not the devil's playground and I will not allow him to play in it."

Soul Food:

Say these statements out loud, when the devil starts playing mind games with you:

- » Excuse me, devil, you are in my way. I've got too much on the to-do list today.
- » Devil, I'm too busy for foolishness today. Sorry. Try someone else.
- » Devil, I am currently unavailable. Please leave me a message with my Father - Jesus.

Soul Work:

Remember it's not just the devil playing mind games, sometimes we are beating ourselves up, in our mind. Say these affirmations when you notice yourself being unkind, in your mind.

- » I will not allow my thoughts to stop the plans God has for me.
- » I will not allow the thoughts in my mind to affect my mood, my feelings, or my decisions.
- » When negative thoughts start to enter my mind I will ask God to take them away so I can focus throughout the day.
- » God can change my thought pattern.
- » This will be an amazing month for me because I will be intentional about what goes in and out of my mind.

DAY 7:

Running on Empty

> *She acknowledges when her cup is getting low and then she makes time to refill it.*

Sister, I don't know why but the words "fill your cup", "fill your cup", and "fill your cup", keep coming to my mind. God is repeating those words to me. Is this God telling me that we need to do a better job at filling our cups? Are you running on empty right now? Are you the sister that always has the word of encouragement to fill your loved ones up, but often stumbles to find the words to fill your cup up? If so, I want us to change that today. Not tomorrow. Not next Sunday or Monday, but today. We have to start being more intentional and observe where our cup levels are. This helps us identify what we need.

I want to introduce you to something that I call a "Check-In". This is an intentional time where you check in with yourself and invite God into your space. You might say to yourself "Hey girl, how are you doing today?", "Where is all this joy coming from today?". You might even say to yourself, "Pause for a moment, you have an attitude, let's unpack where that came from". Checking in with yourself daily has to become your new normal. When you don't reflect daily, you neglect to give room to address the things that are affecting you. You get comfortable feeling unhealthy and run down. This leads us to constantly push feelings away, only to have them eventually come back in front of us.

Honestly, there are days when I don't want to process my feelings, I just want to be mad, sad, and disappointed. I want to continue having my attitude. There is nothing wrong with feeling your feelings. But then you must make time to process those feelings, unpack those feelings, find solutions to those feelings, and then release those feelings.

This check-in doesn't dissolve your problems, but it brings awareness to where you are. It creates room for God to come in and do what only He can do. Life has taught us that we aren't qualified or capable of fixing our own problems. God does a better job at fixing everything that concerns us.

Overflow Jar Activity

Sister, this activity is going to help us fill our cups daily so they don't get empty. Take a moment and find an empty jar at your house preferably a jar that has a lid. Then gather blank paper, note cards, or sticky notes, a pair of scissors, pens, and markers. Once you have all of those items take a moment to set the atmosphere. Play music of your choice: worship, jazz, or a soothing instrumental playlist. Say a prayer and ask God to speak to you, ask God to give you the words to put on the paper.

Now, you're going to pick 50 Bible Verses to write on the paper of your preference and place them in your overflow jar. You can look up Bible verses online, in your Bible, or just reference back to some of your favorites. Choose Bible verses that will encourage you during a hard time and speak directly to your soul.

After you're done picking your Bible Verses now you're going to create 50 affirmations for yourself. What are things you need to hear often? Is it something like "I am breaking generational cycles right now." "God will get me through this". "I need to pause and take a moment to pray". Add a mixture of affirmations to your overflow jar. They can be "I" statements, suggestions of things you need to do, prayers, and maybe even a quote you create for yourself but let the words flow.

Sister, I know there are 365 days in a year but it was intentional that we only started with 100 overflow items in your jar. Each quarter you're going to refill your overflow jar. If you give your Overflow jar a fresh replenishing 4 times a year that means your jar will be overflowing with the overflow. I hope you enjoy this activity!

Your Check-ins don't always have to be centered around processing feelings or flushing through negativity. You're going to have a lot of check-ins that are joy-filled, goal-centered, praise breaks, positive reflections, and a chance to celebrate your growth. Start celebrating your good days, your wins, the miracles that you see, and the baby steps you take to accomplish a bigger goal.

Win Jar Activity

Sister, have you ever had someone share words that truly benefited your life? You know how we are when we find a good bargain, a good resource, a good wig, a good restaurant, some good lashes, or a brunch place to try. We share it with others because we want them to experience it too. I have to give all the credit to one of my sisters. She introduced me to the Win Jar activity.

Grab another jar, a paper of preference, and your pens and markers. Every time you experience a "win" you're going to write it down, add the date, and put it in the jar. After you place your win in the jar, celebrate! Even if it's something as small as saying to yourself "Girl, you did that!". Are you wondering what's considered a win? It is when you didn't curse those folks out, as you wanted to. It is when you eat healthy for the day. It is when you start therapy. A win is taking care of your body and incorporating exercise. A win is when you crushed a goal. A win is when you see a difference in your behavior and attitude in a certain situation. Do I need to go any further, sister? Do you see how you are constantly winning? It's time we keep track of those wins. On days when you feel like you didn't meet the mark or do your best, pull out one of your wins from your win jar to remind yourself that you're still winning, even when you mess up.

Soul Food:

Sister, see how you can incorporate this Bible Verse into your daily life. Take time to reflect on this verse. **Mathew 1:35 (NIV)** says "Very early in the morning, while it was still dark, Jesus got up, left the house, and went off to a solitary place, where he prayed".

Soul Work:

Schedule a time and make it a priority to create your Overflow Jar and Win Jar. Treat yourself to your favorite meal or snack, while you create. Make this an enjoyable time.

DAY 8:

Hustle Culture

She incorporates rest so she can be at her best.

    I admit I am not the best at keeping my cell phone charged. I'm not the sister that you should add to the emergency contact list, because my phone might be dead. I'm trying to get to the root of how my phone dies so often. My phone notifies me with a message every time my phone has a low battery with a notification. In addition, my battery icon will turn red, warning me. I realize that I ignore the signs that tell me my battery is about to die. It's not until I try to make one last phone call that my phone dies mid-sentence, and I realize I ignored all the warning signs.

    I do this same thing when my body tells me, "I need rest." I ignore the indicators telling me "I need a break and I need to pause." I try to ignore how tired I am, but I just keep going. When I should speak up for myself or say no when someone asks me to do something, I often end up saying "yes". Have you ever found yourself there, sister? Ignoring the fatigue, aches, and groans from your body saying "Help me"? Just as our cell phones give us warning signs that our battery is getting low, our body also sends us messages that our capacity is getting low.

I know it's easy to ignore the warning signs because we have so much going on, but I want us to start paying attention. When you realize that your responsibilities are interrupting your rest, that's an indication to pay attention to your body. When that happens, take a moment to restructure some things and strengthen your boundaries.

There have been times when we have gone through our week with little to no energy and nothing real to give. We might become easily irritated because of our lack of rest. We don't intentionally try to be rude or mean to others, but without proper rest, our emotions and feelings can spill out. The littlest things start to annoy us. Why? Because we are tired.

Sister, how can we function properly if we don't take time to recharge? Every week starting Friday night until sunset on Saturday I take time to rest. I don't do any type of work which includes; emails, projects, or work calls. I truly try to unplug. Some weeks I sleep in, or go to church, spend time in nature, enjoy family and friends, or just stay in my pajamas. Anything that helps me completely rest I do my best to incorporate it. Sister, I want you to pick a day that you can rest. A day you can slow things down for 24 hours or just a few hours if you can't do the full 24. Call it your recharge day.

Daily rest is also vital. The recommended amount of hours of sleep per night is 8 hours. Our bodies function better when we get all of our rest.

If Jesus took time to rest from all that He was doing, I know He wants us to incorporate rest too. When we are recharged and rested, goals and dreams become clearer, our work ethic strengthens, and consistency shows up in everything we do. Is your battery running low? Do you need to recharge?

Soul Food:
Sister, take a moment to pause. You've been carrying a lot on your shoulders. Meet God right where you are. Connect with this verse in your own unique way. "Come to me, all of you who are tired from carrying heavy loads, and I will give you rest". ***Mathew 11:28 (GNT)***

Soul Work:
Take a moment and ask yourself these two important questions.   »   Sis, I want you to look at your schedule and I need you to eliminate one thing that is starting to burn you out. It has to go.

> » Have you been getting your 8 hours of sleep? Plan how you will start going to bed earlier. Rest is so important, our bodies need it.

DAY 9:

Gut Check

She is aware that what she puts inside of her system produces what will come out of her system.

One of the sayings I would hate to hear people say was "Your food is your fuel". I only hated it because I am a big foodie. I love a good brunch, a tasty lunch, and a delightful dinner. I love to eat snacks and if sweets are in my sight, I'm eating them too. I just have to be honest, sister. Are you a foodie too? What's your favorite meal? Do you like Chick-fil-A? I love their nuggets and fries with the Polynesian sauce. If I'm having a really good day, I love to celebrate with a milkshake on the side. See how quickly I got off track because we're talking about food. That's how much food excites me!

A few years ago I noticed that I was having really low energy. I would get all of my recommended hours of sleep but I was still so tired throughout the day. The tiredness started to turn into a lack of motivation and then that led to procrastination. I couldn't help but wonder why my body always felt so sluggish and weighed down. I kid you not, it almost felt like God came down from heaven and said "Najma your body keeps shutting down because you will eat a box of Mike and Ike's filled with sugar and that sugar weighs you down". "You then throw a frozen pizza in the oven and eat that and say you ate dinner". "You didn't incorporate any fruits and vegetables, just pizza and Mike and Ike's". "Where are your nutrients?" I'm like, "God but it tastes good, He said I know everything that tastes good isn't good for you".

There I was with a little attitude because God showed me the hard truth. God then sent two angels into my life that taught me about healthy eating. At first, I didn't believe them but then when they let me taste their food, my oh my. That was the game changer for me trying fresh vegan and vegetarian foods that tasted like the meal I had been missing all my life. I didn't understand how something tasted like chicken that wasn't chicken. It was just a healthier version. See sister, I am a flexitarian. Some days I am vegan, other days I'm vegetarian, and some days I eat meat. I like to flex with what I'm eating.

One day I was going to dinner with one of my sisters and she called and said "Hey, I'm picking the restaurant. Are you vegan, vegetarian, or eating meat today"? That's when I knew my flexitarian ways were real, and I couldn't help but laugh. I grew up in a household where my parents didn't serve pork or beef. To this day, I've never had pork or beef. I can't relate when people talk about cheeseburgers, steaks, or pork chops. I've always been curious to know what those foods taste like. Sister, just because I didn't eat pork or beef didn't make me healthy. Eating lots of junk food, processed food, and fast food was killing my body on the inside.

The light bulb really hit me when I attended this health seminar that talked about the power of fruits and vegetables, and how they can heal our bodies. I learned how a lot of diseases like diabetes, cancer, strokes, and high blood pressure can be connected to the foods we eat. It may not be the leading factor but it is a big contributor. Fruits and vegetables are our medicine, sister. They can heal us better than pills. Let's take a moment to pause and reflect because the health topic can be sensitive. I know it was for me because it's like a mirror for me and I saw all the wrong choices I was making regarding my health. Don't let this be that time where you beat yourself up sister instead say this "My body is about to feel completely better because I am about to make some health changes".

Since we cleared the air in the room, ask yourself these questions: Have I been making the right food choices for my body? Has my body been feeling sluggish and weighed down? Could I do better with choosing healthier food options? Do I need a little bit more information on the right foods I should eat in my everyday life? Sister, as you know, I am not a doctor or a scientist but trust that I felt the difference in my body when I cut back on the junk and processed food. I replaced those things and incorporated more fruits, veggies, healthier vegetarian meats, and clean meat, at times. I even started juicing and making smoothies. This forced me to set boundaries within my daily eating habits. Sister, I am also learning how to cook. I never thought I would be able to make healthy meals that I would actually enjoy, because there was a time when I didn't like the meals I cooked. I'm just going to leave that right there. Now, I am starting to enjoy the meals I prepare. Thank you, God.

Now I have a better understanding why I often times felt depressed. I started putting the pieces to the puzzle together. The nights I didn't sleep well were because I ate heavy meals right before I went to sleep. I didn't give my body the chance to process the food I had eaten. My attitude some mornings would have been better if I had eaten a healthy breakfast. It is still hard for me to this day, sister, to maintain healthy eating habits, but my body always reminds me when I get off track. Can we be accountability partners and promise each other that we will be open to trying healthier foods and implementing them into our daily life? I think it's time for us to change our eating pallet. It's time for our taste buds to experience a new taste.

Sister, I believe that we are walking into a new season. I am convinced that God is about to take us higher, stretch us wider, and give us a glimpse of the miracles He has for us. I believe that this season will be more clear and more purposeful if we lean into becoming healthier versions of ourselves. This will begin when we start making healthier food choices. Our bodies will thank us for this in the long run.

Soul Food:

Say this prayer with me, sister. Let's start our prayer with **1 Corinthians 10:31 (NLT)**. "So whether you eat or drink, or whatever you do, do it all for the glory of God".

God, help me to be mindful of what I put in my body. Please, help me develop a love for healthy foods and bring healing to my body. God, please help me to focus on healthy lifestyle changes, rather than a week-long change. Take over my taste buds, Oh Lord! Take over my mind when I want to rush to sweets, fast food options, and unhealthy snacks. Please, introduce me to healthier things to cook, different fruits and vegetables to purchase, and give me creative ways to eat healthier on a daily basis. Amen.

Soul Work:

Sister, here is a suggestion guide to get you started on a healthier eating lifestyle! These are things that helped me when I began my transition to healthier eating (Which is always a work in progress).

- » Take a moment to research the health benefits of these vegetables: Broccoli, Kale, Spinach, Carrots, Celery, Cauliflower, Green Peas, String Beans, and Peppers. Purchase fresh vegetables as much as possible. Canned vegetables have a lot of processed chemicals inside of them that aren't good for our bodies.

» Take a moment to research the health benefits of these fruits: Pineapple, Apples, Watermelon, Yellow and Red Mangoes, Avocados, Passion Fruit, Dragon Fruit, Grapefruit, Oranges, Lemons, Blackberries, and Pomegranates.

» If you find yourself saying "I can't get off of meat sister." Please know that I am not trying to convince you to let go of meat. I just want you to try a few vegetarian options. Remember we are allowing our taste buds to experience something new. To be honest, all vegetarian alternative options aren't healthy. It is important to read the food labels to know what nutrients are inside the foods so you can determine what is best for your overall health. Knowing how much sugar, salt, and saturated fat are contained in your foods is beneficial information to have. Here are some brands to try: Impossible, Morning Star, Beyond Meat, Woringthon, Loma Linda, and Just Egg. Even with these brands, you'll have to read the food labels.

» Sister, what about smoothies? Always add fresh fruits and kale or spinach to your smoothie. It makes a huge difference. Smoothie packs are also good to add to your smoothies. I love this brand called Pitaya Foods because of it's health benefits and wonderful taste. They are filled with antioxidants, probiotics, and natural sweeteners. They have all types of natural smoothie packs. Pop the smoothie pack in the blender, add your fruits, and vegetables, and water or fresh juice, and let it do the magic for you. Research Chia seeds and Flax seeds when you get a chance, sister. I add those two things to my smoothies and they add a great amount of nutrients. You can also get creative and find healthy smoothie recipes. Sister, I also hope you can try juicing. Juicing has now become a part of my weekly schedule. Get a juicer when you can, and find some healthy juicing recipes. Your body is going to fall in love with you all over again.

» Sister, now you know I love a good snack. What I enjoy now is cutting up fruit for the week. I love the weeks when I cut up watermelon and pineapple. Make yourself a big fruit bowl and eat off of the fruit for the week. I also enjoy getting fresh broccoli, cauliflower, and peppers and dipping them with some dairy-free ranch. Hummus makes my tummy smile too. I'm telling you, sister, it's a good day when I do that.

DAY 10:

Keep It Moving

She understands the importance of body mobility. If she is mobile now she will be mobile in the future.

    Sister, if I can be honest I have a weird relationship in my life that's been going on for years. Some days I want to be bothered with the relationship and other days I don't. Some days I want to spend time together and others days I just want to be with myself. Then I stop checking in for months and by that time I feel like I have abandoned the relationship. Can you guess what relationship this is in my life? It is my relationship with the gym. This is the most inconsistent and uncomfortable relationship I've ever been in, perhaps because it pulls me out of my comfort zone and forces me to do things I don't feel like doing. At the same time, I feel good when I do my part in the relationship. It's one of those love-hate relationships. It's like how I hate when my legs are rubbing together and burning in the gym but, I love the accomplishment of finishing the workout right after. How is your relationship with the gym, sister? I am learning that the root of the problem in this relationship boils down to my discomfort with exercising.

I almost feel like me and the gym should go to therapy because we have some issues to resolve. This back-and-forth has to stop. If I weigh the pros and cons of this relationship, the pros win. I feel so much better when my body is moving and getting exercise. There is a lift in my mood and energy levels. I become more confident in other areas of my life. The American Heart Association recommends that we workout at least 150 minutes per week. That's five 30-minute workouts per week. That doesn't mean that each of the workouts has to be intense. That can mean going for a walk, swimming, attending a Zumba class or cycling class, or a workout at home. Exercise doesn't always look like "going to the gym".

There is another reason why I had an attitude in the relationship. I felt like I always had to travel to see the gym. It felt one-sided. But the truth is, I can bring the gym home to me. It may look different because I don't have all the equipment but I can have the same mindset I have in the gym. That mindset is pushing through even when it feels uncomfortable, especially when my body starts aching. I remind myself that there is a greater benefit for my body down the road, stemming from the choices I make today. A little discomfort is going to be a blessing along the way.

Sister, right now I'm not talking about our weight, or the dream bikini for this summer, or the dress we want to wear for our birthday. All those things are great but I'm talking about a lifestyle change. I'm talking about a better relationship with our bodies. I'm talking about us giving our temple the love and care it needs to function properly. We've got to break the toxic cycle with exercise. Only exercising when we want to see a certain result and then going back to our old habits. That's not going to be beneficial to us in the long run.

Let's make those adjustments now. Sister, let's practice walking every day for 30 minutes. Let's get out of our comfort zone for a minute and sign up for the group exercise class. Maybe you need to invest in a personal trainer. If working out at home is more convenient for you, YouTube and other programs have so many free and accessible workouts. Let's fall in love with our bodies and daily exercise. This change isn't going to happen overnight. It happens with small steps. Are you willing to take a step, sister? One step turns into forward movement. The movement may feel uncomfortable or exhausting. However, our bodies need daily movement. Let's give our bodies what it needs. We can do this sister!

Soul Food:

Take a moment to dissect what this verse means to you. Journal your response.

"Don't you realize that your body is the temple of the Holy Spirit, who lives in you and was given to you by God? You do not belong to yourself, for God bought you at a high price. So you must honor God with your body".
1 Corinthians 6: 19-20 (NLT)

Soul Work:

Sister, when you get a moment go to the "Center of Disease and Prevention (CDC)" website. It gives us insight on the benefits of daily exercise.

- » Daily exercise improves brain health. Sister, we need a healthy brain. Lord, knows I do.
- » Daily exercise helps maintain a healthy weight.
- » Daily exercise helps prevent diseases.
- » Daily exercise helps strengthen our bones and muscles.
- » Daily exercise helps us with daily movement and mobility.

Day 11:

Is Therapy for Me?

She uses therapy as her tool to help renew her mind and soul.

Sister, one thing you have to know about me is my love for travel. I am always ready to book a trip. If it's a nice location, has yummy food, and some relaxation is incorporated, then you can count me in. As much as I love traveling, one thing that I dislike is packing. I normally wait until the night before to pack. You would think by the way I countdown the days until the trip it would give me a sense of urgency to pack. It never happens that way. If I can be honest, packing somewhat stresses me out. I'm constantly wondering if I am packing too much or packing too little. Having to think about what I am going to wear for the next few days makes me exhausted. Once I start the packing process, I pile up way too much and my "carry-on bag" begins to feel and look like a "checked bag".

I typically have items packed in my suitcase that I am probably not going to wear. Then, I arrive at my destination with a full suitcase and an almost broken arm because my bags were so heavy. Days go by on my trip and I am constantly reminded that I brought many things that I do not need.

As I thought more and more about this, I realized this is how we approach life. We carry past baggage with us everywhere we go. Stuff we didn't even realize we were carrying for so long. We tote it from place to place, year after year. We carry things with us from our childhood to our adulthood, and from one relationship to the next. We do this as women because we were taught to always be strong. We are often looked down on when we cry or we express how something made us feel. There may have been other times when we weren't allowed to speak up about the things that happened to us. You might have grown up hearing the words, "What happens in this house stays in this house," or "Don't share our business." We are taught to keep going physically but internally our mind and soul are screaming "Help".

When I found out I was pregnant as a teenage girl my soul was crying "Help me", but I didn't know what help looked like. My family was there for me and I even had some close friends by my side but I needed more. The pain I was feeling couldn't just be drenched in prayer. Don't get me wrong, prayer is amazing. Prayer is a powerful tool that connects us to God in an intimate way, and it also gives us access to all of Heaven's resources. Prayer should be our first stop for guidance before we seek anything but sometimes we need something immediately after prayer. I believe that tool is therapy.

I want you to know that it was not your fault that someone molested you when you were a child. It was not your fault that you didn't have a mother or father figure in your life growing up. It was not your fault that someone raped you and took your innocence away. I know sometimes you blame yourself but it wasn't your fault that some things happened to you. You may be wondering why this is still affecting you when it happened so long ago. It's still affecting you because you never got a chance to unpack it, you just left it inside. You have been moving along in life rolling a heavy suitcase that is ready to be unpacked and filled with new things.

Let's start unpacking. You might have experienced horrible relationships and you are still trying to recover. Let's unpack that. You might have had an abortion and you don't know how to forgive yourself. Let's unpack that. You might have lost a close family member and you are still grieving. Let's unpack that. You might have lost your home or gone bankrupt and you feel like a failure. Let's unpack that, sister. You might still be upset with yourself for having sexual encounters with a man that was married. Can you forgive yourself and know God forgives you and unpack that? You might be struggling with feeling lonely and depressed and you don't know where those feelings are coming from. Let's unpack that. Your credit score might make you sick because of your past decisions. Let's unpack that. I want us to consider unpacking these things in therapy. I want us to have a safe space to talk with someone and let loose all the things that are tied up.

    Sister, I have to say this. I am only saying this because we are sisters. We can't keep going back to drugs, alcohol, sex, and other devices that bring us temporary pleasure. We need to experience something that gives us a lasting effect that leads us to healing. We want to be healed, and not just wear a temporary band-aid that we have to keep replacing. We are experiencing deep pain. It's time for us to release that pain. It's time for us to unpack the things that hurt us because we are carrying them with us everywhere we go. It is starting to affect our workplace, our children, our relationships, and our growth. When things happen to us we have to take time to heal and process what happened. Keeping everything inside hurts our souls. We can't grow if we don't take time to process things. This means we are going to have to revisit some things that we have dismissed. Yes, I know that's hard revisiting pain but we have to heal.

    So what does this look like? How do I heal from pain? Sister, I'm not going to lie, I have experienced some things in my life that have bruised me. I started to realize how I was blaming everything on everyone because of my pain. It was starting to affect the way I treated people. I was either irritated or feeling depressed. At that time in my life, I didn't understand what counseling and therapy was. I kept thinking I'm not about to tell a stranger all of my secrets. How are they going to help me when they don't even know me?

    Then, I felt God interrupting my negative thoughts and all the excuses I was making about not trying therapy. "Najma they are going to be able to help you and give you tools because they have been trained in this area". "You're right, they are a stranger and that's why they won't judge you". You should be more concerned if it was someone you knew. I then had my "Okay, God" moment. "I'll try this". I then started to pray, remembering that prayer comes first. I started praying and asking God if He could lead me to the right therapist. I asked God if He could help me be open to sharing things I've never shared with anyone.

    I didn't just want any therapist, I wanted the right therapist for me. My preference was to have someone that mixed therapy and faith in God. I knew if we combined the right tools and invited God to play His part in the sessions, I would be more open. As you are praying and asking God for a therapist you may not know what your preference is, and that's okay. Just lean in and ask God for help.

    I was still feeling uneasy about the whole "going to therapy" thing. God started showing me how He wants me to be in His word to heal, but He also wants me to trust the resources He has placed on this earth to help me. One of those transformational resources is therapy. I finally got myself together and started looking up therapists and asking for recommendations. I couldn't find anything. I then started to think "See maybe this isn't for me".

    It wasn't until I attended a workshop and just so happened a therapist was the presenter. She slayed that workshop up and down. Sister, she did that! She was discussing triggers and trauma and how they affect our daily life. After the session, someone bravely asked, "Are you accepting any new clients". I was too afraid to ask. She answered, "Yes I am now accepting new clients". Her bold question opened a door for my healing. Immediately after the workshop I went to her website and signed up for my first therapy session. Your sister was scared but I am happy to share that I have been working with my therapist for over three years and we still have work to do. Why, because I am a work in progress and I have accepted that.

Sister, take it from me. Therapy is soul-changing. Therapy is mind-changing. Therapy is generational cycle-breaking. Therapy is a tool that helps you discover the woman you were created to be.

Sister, whether you need to meet with someone weekly, biweekly, or monthly just try it. If you had a therapist and it didn't work out, then ask God to help you find another one. I never thought I would find my therapist attending a workshop. Remember, it doesn't matter how young you are or how seasoned you are to begin therapy.

As women, we need an outlet because we all have experienced some type of trauma. Whether it was in our childhood or as an adult. Something is inside of us that needs to be unpacked. Don't put your pain on hold any longer. It's time for you to unpack, release, and heal.

Soul Food:

Take some time to meditate on **Proverbs 19:20 (GNT)** "If you listen to advice and are willing to learn, one day you will be wise". Keep this verse close to you.

Soul Work:

Sister, would you be interested in trying therapy or going back to therapy? Psychology Today is a wonderful website that helps you find a therapist in your area. Pray and ask God to send you the right therapist. The cost of therapy should not be the reason why you can't go. Check and see what health insurance benefits you have for therapy and there are also so many free resources. There might be some in your area. Take time to do some research and consider all of your options.

Day 12:

Sister! Sister!

She is learning how to cultivate new relationships because she is becoming a healthier woman.

    A lot of times when I was growing up I had a hard time keeping friendships. Having healthy relationships in my life wasn't common for me. Maybe because I didn't have many examples where healthy relationships were modeled. There were times in my life when I would observe women at church be kind one minute and then whisper about a sister the next minute. As a child, you mimic what you see, and I brought those same behaviors into my relationships with me.

    I brought gossip into relationships with me. I brought unkindness into the relationships I was forming. I brought unrealistic expectations to each friendship I made. Everyone was the problem but me. "They aren't loyal". "They don't have my back". "I don't trust them". These sentences were on repeat from one friendship to the next. Here I was searching for the right friendship but also carrying baggage with me, everywhere I went.

Did you grow up like me, sister? Not seeing the healthiest relationships between women? As children, we mimicked the behavior, but as adults, we can change the behavior. We can change the way we view sisterhood. We can change the way we interact with other sisters. We can break the curse of having unhealthy relationships. I am learning that true sisterhood is good for the soul. It's the seasoning that you never want to get rid of.

Have you ever had a moment where God showed you that you were the problem? That was me, sister. God had to show me that I was the problem in several of my friendships. I was pointing the finger at the other person but the finger was pointing back at me and almost sticking me in the eye saying "It's you". When I finally realized that truth it hurt me to my core. Hurt people hurt people… I was taking the hurt I was experiencing into each of my relationships.

A few years ago I couldn't admit this, but I thank God for therapy and self-awareness now. Can I get an amen, sister? My friendships have drastically changed, because I started looking within. I couldn't look to the left or the right anymore. I had to look right in front of me and that image was me. I had to face myself. Take a moment and look at you. How are you in friendships? How do you treat your sisters? Do you share her secrets with others? Do you place unrealistic expectations on your friendships? Have you brought your hurt and pain into relationships unintentionally? Do you often get upset over the littlest things in your friendships? What is an area you can improve?

All relationships require maintenance. Relationships are intentional work because no human is perfect. Both individuals will make mistakes within the relationship. Mistakes aren't one-sided. Since mistakes aren't one-sided, both people have to accept that there will be times when the other person needs some additional grace.

One more thing that's ruining sisterhood is expecting your sister to do what you would do. Expecting her to handle the situation the same way you would handle the situation. God built the two of you differently; you weren't supposed to respond the same way to things. You were meant to be different. Embrace your sister's uniqueness and love the differences that the two of you share. Just because she doesn't give gifts the way you give gifts does not classify her as not a good friend. Just because she doesn't stand up for you the way you stand up for her doesn't mean she isn't a good friend. You both just have different approaches to how you handle situations.

Healthy sisterhood is vital. We weren't meant to live life alone, sister. That is why I love the She Can Movement, because we are a group of sisters that walk through life together. Encouraging one another, supporting one another, helping one another, and watching each other walk into whatever it is God has for us. With that said, sister, can you give sisterhood another chance? Can you give sisters in your hometown another chance? Can we set an example of what it looks like to be an imperfect sister and friend? Let's release some of the ideas that sisterhood only is messy, full of gossip, and filled with jealousy and unkindness. Let's change that narrative. You may not have had the best relationships but you can begin again and cultivate a new sisterhood with new sisters.

Soul Food:

I pray that you find a sister that can sharpen your iron as well as you sharpen hers. "Just as iron sharpens iron, friends sharpen the minds of each other". **Proverbs 27:17 (CEV)**

Soul Work:

Let's take some time to get in a quiet space and pray about sisterhood. Here are three prayers for you to pray.

> » **OPEN HEART PRAYER:** Sister, in this prayer make room to have an open heart. Make room to come out of your comfort zone. I know you might be healing from hurtful relationships and perhaps you're not quite ready to open back up. You might be saying to yourself, I have enough sisters. You could be nervous about inviting new sisters into your space. Wherever you are, be vulnerable. Ask God to help you to open up to your new sisters,

whenever He brings them in your path. Ask God to align you with the right sister so you can be a blessing to one another and help each other grow.

» **TRANSFORMATION PRAYER:** Sister, in this prayer be as vulnerable and authentic as you can. During the transformation prayer, you are praying for yourself. Ask God to teach you how to become a better sister. A sister that communicates well, encourages, supports, is loyal, is open, is a listener, and provides helpful feedback. Then take a moment and ask God to help you remove jealousy, comparison, or anything else from your heart that may arise in a friendship.

» **REMOVAL PRAYER:** Sister, this prayer is always tough. Take time to ask God to remove any friendships from your life that shouldn't be there anymore. During this prayer, ask God to help you part ways with those relationships that you have outgrown.

DAY 13:

Bad Breath

> *She realizes that God is concerned about the words she speaks.*

There was this period in my life when I was experiencing very bad breath. Sister, I promise you I was flossing, brushing my teeth morning, night, and in between. I was going to get my teeth cleaned. At one point I needed to get a tooth pulled so I thought that would fix it. Nothing worked sister. It was honestly embarrassing. I didn't even want to talk with people. One day, I felt the holy spirit saying "I had to do something to keep your mouth shut". I realized during that period in my life I was gossiping so much. I had all the tea. I wanted all the tea. Finally, God had to shut me up so I couldn't say anything. What an embarrassing way to get my attention but sometimes God has to do what He has to do to get us to listen to Him.

Sister, I promise I've gotten better so if you see me now and my breath smells like onions, just know I love onions on most things, so give me a breath mint. I share this uncomfortable season with you because I believe it is important that we are mindful of the conversations we are having. We have to be more careful about the words we are saying about others.

During that time I realized I wasted so much time gossiping, and ignoring what God was asking me to do. It was a lesson I had to learn. I realized during a heavy season of gossiping I was unhappy with myself. I was unhappy with the relationships I was experiencing. I was unhappy with myself for having an abortion. I was unhappy with some of the ways my life had unfolded. At that time, it was easier and safer for me to take the attention off of myself and my pain and focus it on others.

God switched it all around with bad breath that shut me up. Sister, I know gossip can feel fun, and juicy, and some days exciting to get all the information. Think about how much time gossiping takes from your day. The hour you spent on the phone you could have been doing something else you love. Also, gossip doesn't change the person or the outcome of the situation, it is "small talk" that's not beneficial. Sister, we are better than that. We are better than talking about our other sisters. We are better than talking about our family members and people on our job. We are better than keeping up with the latest church drama.

God is ready to fill the time that you spend gossipping with the things He has called you to do. God is ready to use that time to give you a new vision and perspective about things in your life that are about to change. Sister, gossiping doesn't even fit you well. You love others, you care about this world, and you want change, just like me. I know you want change, because you have this book.

It's time that you set communication boundaries with some people in your life. They may be shocked that they can't stay on the phone for hours with you anymore rehearsing the same things about your family or your situation. You might have to ignore some phone calls because you already know the outcome of the conversation. Start praying that God sends the right people in your life to have positive conversations with. You want conversations that bring fruit into your life. You want positive and good fruit in your life. You don't want discord, messy fruit, or molded fruit. It's crazy to think now how God can transform my words and the way I speak. I am still working on this daily and I fall short some days. It just amazes me that I now get annoyed about gossip. I'll even try to change the subject when it comes my way. And I'm still shocked when I remember the impact it had on my life.

Each time you are confronted with gossip, take a moment to shut it down and switch gears within the conversation. Advocate for the person that is being gossiped about. You can walk away or find a way to ignore it. We can't change other people but we have a responsibility to God to change our own behavior.

Soul Food:

Here are some Bible verses that help me to this day when it comes to the words I speak, gossiping, and monitoring my conversations.

- » "Take control of what I say, O LORD, and guard my lips". ***Psalm 141:3 (NLT)***
- » "Sharp words cut like a sword, but words of wisdom heal". ***Proverbs 12:18 (CEV)***
- » "Do not use harmful words, but only helpful words, the kind that build up and provide what is needed, so that what you say will do good to those who hear you". ***Ephesians 4:29 (GNT)***
- » "Kind words are like honey— sweet to the soul and healthy for the body". ***Proverbs 16:24 (NLT)***

Soul Work:

Sister, take a moment to write about how you have been using your words lately. Have you found yourself gossipping more than usual? Who is the person you generally gossip with most? How can you change the conversations you have with the person? Ask God to help you with the words that you speak.

DAY 14:

Unrooting Comparison

> *She embraces there is no duplication of her. God only created one of her.*

There is no one like you. I mean absolutely no one. God didn't duplicate you in any form. He made you in His own way. For that reason, no one can do things like you. The way you do things is unique. It's so unique that sometimes people don't understand why you operate in such a way. You and God met when you were in your mother's womb. What an intimate place to meet God, the place you were being formed and created. God was creating you and strategically developing you. He was creating you differently than the people that already existed on Earth. He didn't want you to be like anyone else that was here.

That's why He took His time with you. He needed you here on earth.

Sister, while you were in your mother's womb God was numbering the days of your life. He started designing your gifts and your talents. He knew the things that would interest and not interest you. He was being very careful when He was designing you. That's why when you came out of your mother's womb you were a beautiful soul that the world had never seen before. The way your eyes opened was different, your cry was different, and my goodness, your smile was different.

Everything about you is wonderfully different. It's intentional why God created you differently. It has everything to do with your purpose and why you were brought into this world. Nothing about you is a mistake, it's all a part of God's plan. Take a moment to get comfortable with yourself and the way you were created. Take time to look in the mirror. Look at the beauty, the scars, the gifts you bring, and the insecurity you always hide. I hope while you're looking at yourself you see a beautiful imperfect masterpiece. A daughter to the most powerful man in the whole wide world.

In the world we live in today, it's hard to accept the way we were created. Our days are consumed with trying to change ourselves rather than accepting ourselves. I want you to own your differences. Own the uniqueness about you. Get comfortable with who you are and who you were created to be.

Comparison can rob our identity and have us question who God intended for us to be. Comparison will make you feel like you are behind and others are ahead. Comparison will have you wondering what your place is in this ever-changing world. Sister, since you are in this world that means you belong here.

I know you see other people's lives captured through a lens, but you never know what's happening when the flash is off. There's a reason why God didn't make your life like there's. Trust me He was being strategic. There's a reason why He hasn't introduced you to your spouse yet. It's hard to understand because you see others around you with their spouse. You're wondering why everyone around you is getting promoted and you can't help but think, "Why not me?" It's okay to feel that way, but God is gearing you up for a promotion that your eyes haven't seen before.

Guard your eyes from what you think your life should look like right now. You're exactly where you're supposed to be in this season of your life. Detox all roots of comparison out of your soul. What your sister has in her life right now is for her, and what you have is for you. What your siblings have in their life is their destiny and God is leading you to yours. What your co-workers experience is their business, God wants you to focus on yours. Your relationships in life can be healthier if you accept that you are different people, with different journeys, and different outcomes. God's blessings don't look the same. All of His blessings look different. Seeing how God blesses someone else shouldn't make you want to compare. It should give you hope.

The root of comparison can stop today if you accept that you were designed by God for a divine purpose, bigger than the idea you have in your head. I know fleeing from comparison is hard. It's easier to look to the side to see what's happening around you through others, but God is calling you to look straight ahead because you then will see all He has for you.

Soul Food:

Let this verse heal any wound you are trying to patch. "And I praise you because of the wonderful way you created me. Everything you do is marvelous! Of this I have no doubt".
Psalm 139:14 (CEV)

Soul Work:

Here are four affirmations you can say to yourself when comparison tries to creep in.

- » God formed me differently and since He formed me differently my life will look different from others.
- » I am right where I am supposed to be. I am not behind and I am not too far ahead. God made no mistakes with me.
- » God blesses everyone in different forms. My blessing is coming; it will just look different from what I've seen before.
- » I accept that my life won't look like anyone else's life. I am excited about living a life I have never seen before.

DAY 15:

Soul Maintenance

> *She is reminded that maintenance isn't just required for her car but also for her soul.*

After driving many miles, our car eventually needs some form of maintenance. Sometimes that maintenance is an oil change, a tire rotation, or a headlight being replaced. If we delay the maintenance service, our car will not operate at its best capabilities. We have to find time within our busy schedule to take our car to get serviced. We rarely delay because our vehicle is important to us. We have places to be, people to see, and things to do.

The same way we make car maintenance appointments a priority, we have to schedule appointments for our soul. This is called soul maintenance. Taking much-needed intentional time for our soul. Soul maintenance is different from rest. Soul maintenance is making time to do things you are passionate about and actively putting yourself in environments that nourish your soul.

When was the last time or have you ever treated yourself with a ticket to attend a women's conference? An environment where you can be around other women. A place where you can receive inward maintenance and a soul tune-up. Women's conferences have a way of setting a tone, not just while you are in the room, but also that you carry forward as you leave. Your mind is refreshed, your soul is more at ease, and you're more clear about the direction God is taking you. Your environment is key when it comes to soul maintenance. Women's Conferences are a place where you arrive ready to pour out but you leave filled up.

Have you invested in going to a training or taking a class? Particularly to study something you've always wanted to do but just didn't have the bandwidth to do it. Has your favorite author had a book tour and you somehow have always missed the event? Have you ever been curious about how to make something? Maybe it's attending a candle-making class, a t-shirt-making course, or learning the skill of flower arrangements. Each time the workshop becomes available you say "I'll attend next time". Every time you delay digging into your God-given passions, your soul misses the chance to operate at its fullest potential.

Don't block what God is trying to present to you. God gives us wisdom and vision each time we practice soul maintenance because when we give our soul the maintenance it needs, things become clearer. Dreams translate into small action goals. Visions turn into execution. Make a point to be intentional about soul maintenance. If it's attending something quarterly that feeds your soul, do it. Put some funds to the side so you can invest in yourself. One month it might be attending a conference, the next month it might be attending a comedy show, or maybe you need a staycation or a solo trip. Your soul maintenance will look different each time depending on your need, but make it a priority to schedule it.

Soul Food:

"My soul thirsts for God, for the living God. When can I go and meet with God"? **Psalm 42:2 (NIV)**

Soul Work:

Psalm 42:2 asks a question, "When can I go and meet with God"? Plan a time for soul maintenance and reflect on that question.

DAY 16:

Resetting Love

She might have wounds that hurt but she still operates from a place of love. Wounds no longer dictate the way she loves.

    Love can be a sensitive word for me, then there are other times where I want to operate in love and show love. I can't lie, sister, it's hard for me to love people that have hurt me. Why do I want to love someone that doesn't ultimately love me? It's something I struggle with. It wasn't until my senior year in college, I was in one of my social work classes at Oakwood University and my professor Dr. Ashley showed our class these scriptures in 1 Corinthians. After reading those verses I started looking at love in a different light. It was almost like these verses gave me a sense of relief because I felt like I could actually love.

Sister, let's reconnect with the word "love" and practice what it means. Let's learn differently than we've been taught before. Instead of hearing "love your neighbor: forgive others and love them, wear love on your neck and operate in it at all times." Those sayings are great but let's look beyond them. 1 Corinthians teaches us how to love in a very practical way. It teaches us what love is and what love is not. Sister, go with me for a moment to 1 Corinthians 13: 4-8. Allow this verse to go inside your roots and speak to your mind and soul. Allow this verse to bring comfort to all of your love scars that are progressively healing.

"Love is patient and kind. Love is not jealous or boastful or proud or rude. It does not demand its own way. It is not irritable, and it keeps no record of being wronged. It does not rejoice about injustice but rejoices whenever the truth wins out. Love never gives up, never loses faith, is always hopeful, and endures through every circumstance. Prophecy and speaking in unknown languages and special knowledge will become useless. But love will last forever". (NLT)

Sister, how does this verse make you feel when you read about love in this way? Does it feel more attainable and more realistic? It still feels hard for me, but it helps me brainstorm and create ways I can operate in love. Sister, I pray that God heals you in every area that you feel like you can't love again. I pray He fills your heart, your mind, and your soul with love. I pray that love comes to you and it follows you wherever you go. I pray that people see and feel love every time they encounter you.

Soul Food:

Sister, grab your journal and try to find a quiet place to write. You're going to be writing about love. How it makes you feel, your love wounds, and people you need to love more. Write what **1 Corinthians 13:4-8** means to you and how you can start incorporating practical ways to show love.

Soul Work:

Sister, here are some acts of love we can show to others! Incorporate some of these love challenges as you go through life. Love is intentionally going to start following you everywhere you go.

- » Pick a day each week to give 4 genuine compliments to another person. You will discover how you're going to progressively begin to give daily compliments, more naturally.
- » The next time you're in a drive-through line, picking up your food, pay for the person's food in front of you or behind you. This is truly going to make their day. This challenge might take you out of your comfort zone.

- Do you have any extra clothes in your closet that you don't wear anymore? What about donating them to someone you know in need or giving them to a local organization that could benefit from them? What a beautiful way of showing love.
- Take a moment to bless people that oftentimes don't receive much appreciation for all the hard work they do. You can get creative with this challenge! What about taking thank you cards to the custodians in your local school district? You can add a piece of candy to the card or a word of encouragement. How about taking roses to the maids and cleaners at hotels? You could give each of them a rose to show appreciation. Give to a waitress or host at a local restaurant. Maybe you could take some baked goods. Think of ways to show love creatively to people that aren't shown love often.

DAY 17:

Parental Trauma

She accepts that trauma is not her responsibility but her healing is her responsibility.

    Do you ever have moments in your life where you sit and reflect on your childhood? It might not be an everyday reflection but have there been times when your mind just wondered? Wondered why. You might question if there was a reason why you weren't taught some things at a certain age. Then there may be times when you're still trying to figure out why you were exposed to things that you should have been shielded from. When you pause you may realize that you have many questions about your childhood that you haven't received the answers to.

    There have been days where I have just sat and wondered "Why this or why that". Wishing that my parents could have provided more in some areas and less in others. One day, God gave me an answer. He helped me look at my parents through a different lens. Not the lens I can see them in now, but the lens when they were growing up and I wasn't alive. God took me through the lens when my mother was a teenage girl and lost her mother at a prime time when her life was just getting ready to begin. At 19 years old, my mother had to return home from college to take care of her mother because she was sick. Then days go by and all of a sudden her mother is gone. I can only imagine how my mother felt lost and displaced trying to navigate a world without the person she called her best friend.

Then God switched the lens and took me into the life of my father. He gave me a glimpse of my father's world, the world when he was a boy growing up in Buffalo New York. He grew up with a strong mother trying to raise 3 boys. She did this by herself, doing the best she could. My grandmother worked several jobs to put my father through school when he was a little boy. She noticed early on that he was a very bright child and he needed to be in a different environment. His intelligence and his ability to play basketball were like a two-for-one special. Here I am imagining my father growing up with a single mother trying to be a leader in the home. He was excelling in school, working hard in basketball, but keeping a close eye on his mother and brothers.

When I come out of this lens, my eyes are watery with streams of tears rolling down my face. All I hear is the word "grace." "Give them grace Najma, your parents did the best they could with what they were taught". "Therapy, family resources, and opportunities weren't common like they are today, extend grace". Here I am today, healing, growing, and extending grace to my parents for doing the best they could with what they had. There wasn't always a time when I called my parents "my best friend". Now, I can count on receiving a message from my dad daily with an encouraging message to keep my head up, a joke to make me scream, or a heartfelt "I love you" from miles away. My mom and I talk on the phone every day, constantly looking for when we can schedule our next vacation together, then we start talking about what we ate for the day, and then we have to tell each other how much we miss each other.

    I went from not understanding my parents to now loving my parents. I went from judging my parents to now extending my parents' grace. I share all this to say, we must gather the courage to look at our parents' lives through a different lens. This requires us to be willing to go through all the feelings that are attached to how we view our parents. Some of us have wounds from our parents that we can't seem to let go because we just don't understand why some things had to happen. We may never get the answer to that question. This quote changed my perspective on the way I view my childhood. "Trauma is not your fault, but your healing is your responsibility". This quote is so deep but also so real. The trauma that you experienced wasn't your fault, sister. Don't blame yourself for things that happened in your childhood. Now, it's your responsibility to begin your healing journey when it comes to addressing trauma in your childhood.

    This is the season to look in a different lens and extend grace to our parents, guardians, and the people that raised us. For some of the things that you may have experienced, you might not want to extend any grace or forgiveness. Sister, I totally understand why. I just want to invite you into the freedom God has for us when we release any unforgiveness we have towards our parents or guardians. It's a different type of freedom. A freedom that reminds you that you are no longer bound by the way you grew up. It's a freedom to walk into breaking generational cycles. It also allows you to teach the next generation behind you about what family systems should really look like in a family.

I don't know your story. I just know the producer of your story, and I know the producer of your story is ready to produce a new level of freedom inside of you. He's ready to produce a change within you. He's ready to produce a new outcome for your life. Will you walk with God and let Him produce all the areas in your life that aren't produced yet? This starts with acknowledging and forgiving people in your childhood. I'm encouraging you to allow God to do an inner healing inside you, and heal places only God has access to. Then God can give you wisdom on what you should do next.

The truth is our parents went through trauma, and their parents went through trauma, and our parent's parents went through trauma too. That leads us to cycles of family trauma. Breaking the generational cycle won't happen overnight, but will happen in small and steady steps. Healing is a continuous journey. A huge change is about to be birthed inside of you and through your actions. Let grace lead you and allow forgiveness to stand in front of you.

Soul Food:

Sister, I am speaking this verse over you. **Philemon 1:25 (NLT)** says "May the grace of the Lord Jesus Christ be with your spirit".

Soul Work:

Sister, take a moment to process and pray about your feelings towards your childhood, your parents, or your guardian. Get quiet and listen so God can speak to you. Allow God to start healing you in every area. God may lead you to talk with a therapist about some of the things you have experienced. Whatever He leads you to do, just be open to His guide. He won't lead you in the wrong direction. God is very sensitive to your situation.

DAY 18:

Mother Nature

She will start spending more time in nature because that's where dreams and ideas bloom.

To this day I recall the time when me, my mother, and my brother lived with my granny in the country, in Virginia. Grandma Ella's house was my favorite place to be. She was my great-grandmother. Between her making cheese toast and lemon pies, my belly was in heaven. She also had a wooden fire stove. Yes, it was the type of stove that you would have to cut down a tree and get the wood for. Real country living, I tell you. Sister, when it was 90 degrees outside Grandma Ella would still have that stove going. We both would wipe our sweat at the top of our heads together. My favorite thing about living at Grandma Ella's house was playing on her well. You know in the country, a lot of houses get their water from outside wells. Let me be clear, she would tell me almost 20 times a day "Najma, don't play on that well", but sister, I couldn't help it. Her well was shaped like a stage, you would have thought I was on a stage in an arena, talking to the trees, singing to the top of my lungs, and being an imaginary school teacher. Teaching my imaginary students was the best part of my day. I would teach them art, math, science, and we always had a spelling bee. Now, I also was the teacher that would say "Stop talking, it's class time, we'll have recess soon". These are the memories I made in nature.

My second favorite thing about Grandma Ella's house was her screened-in porch. We would go out and sit, sing church hymns, pray, and take in the cool breeze. We would soak in the beauty of the rose bushes and the big oak trees. Birds were everywhere and we would tune into the beautiful songs they would sing. The neighbors would drive by beeping their horns and we would throw our hands up and say hi.

When you live in the country, everybody's your family and I mean everybody. You have 800 cousins, 250 aunts, 130 uncles, and 75 godmothers and godfathers. My grandfather was Thomas Jackson and everybody in town called him "Tunny". That was Grandma Ella's son and my mother's father. Every day he would come to Grandma Ella's house. My grandfather loved trucks. He had this big brown truck that you could hear from miles away. When we sat on the porch I would hear his engine coming down the road and I would yell "Papa's coming Papa's coming". And moments later, he would pull into the driveway. God blessed that truck because it always sounded like it was on its last leg, but it kept hanging on. I would run outside and wait for Papa to get out of his truck. My papa would greet me with a "Hello Nazma" he never could say "Najma". I was totally fine with that because I was a grandpa's girl, for sure.

Growing up in the country made me feel like nature was my home. I felt alive and free. The only time I wouldn't go outside is if it was too cold or if it was raining. Even on days when it was cold, my mother would bundle my brother and me up to go play in the snow. We were a beach family too. Every summer my mother would make her way to Dollar Tree to get beach toys so we could make sand castles. We would laugh until this day because the car my mother had at the time was almost like my papa's truck. The only difference was it was on its very last leg. My papa's truck had a few more legs to go. My mother's car had a hole in the bottom and if my mother looked down she would say she could see her engine.

To this day sister, my love for the outdoors remains. I love sitting outside journaling and reading. In the evenings, I go for a walk and just breathe in and breathe out. I love looking at the clouds to see what shapes are forming. The outdoors is my comforting place and part of my healing journey.

Maybe you have been trying to get clarity on areas of life. I wonder if spending time in nature would give your brain the clarity it needs. Or you might just need a day to soak in the clouds, the birds chirping, and allow your eyes to take in all of nature's views.

The short time it takes to get in and out of our cars or a once-a-year family cookout doesn't count, sister. Spending time in nature has to be incorporated into the new season that we are walking in. New seasons require new shifts to take place. In order for this season to be different from last season, something has to shift. Your daily dose of nature has to be a part of the shift. I know it gets hot, cold, and the bugs are everywhere but those things are just distractions to keep us inside. I was doing some research on the impact of nature and I found a study that shared some great benefits of spending time outdoors. Here is some information that I discovered:

- » Spending time in nature increases your feelings of calmness
- » It reduces your levels of irritability
- » It lowers your blood pressure and your cortisol which is your stress hormone.
- » It reduces feelings of isolation
- » It restores your capacity for concentration and attention
- » It increases your endorphin levels which promotes happiness
- » It reduces symptoms of anxiety and depression

I didn't realize there were that many benefits of spending intentional time in nature. If you need additional support in any of the areas they mentioned, see how spending time outdoors will be a positive benefit to you. Just give it a try sister we don't know until we try.

Soul Food:

Let's enjoy all the things God made. "Through him, God made all things; not one thing in all creation was made without Him". ***John 1:3 (GNT)***

Soul Work:

Sister, I'm challenging you to spend some more time outside. Choose a challenge that you want to commit to this quarter. Then next quarter, pick a different challenge. Each quarter, switch it up or incorporate more.

- » Walk for 35 minutes 4 times a week
- » Take 20-30 minutes 3 times a week to journal outside
- » Plant some flowers and spend time with them each day, for at least 15 minutes
- » This might be your time to start a small garden, you'll always be spending time in nature
- » Have a picnic in nature often
- » Sit outside and read for 30 minutes
- » Your body might need some stillness. Sit outside and just listen to the birds chirp, watch the clouds, do mediation exercises, and take in the scenery
- » Take your workout outside, it could be yoga, Zumba, or something you follow along to.

DAY 19:

Activating Spiritual Gifts

> *She listened to God and He said "I formed your gifts when you were in your mother's womb".*

    Sister, today as I am reflecting on Martin Luther King Jr. words and remembering the things he did for our country and I can't help but be thankful. I know that we would not be where we are today if it was not for him. We still have a long way to go but he was a huge instrument in some of the changes that we see today.

    If you think about it, it was dangerous to speak up about injustice during the time Martin Luther King was leading and advocating. Being a bold speaker during that time cost something. The cost was possibly risking your life, putting your family in danger, and losing everything connected to you.

Martin Luther King Jr. was a brilliant leader and always had God by his side. Did you know that he also was a minister? People may think that's crazy being an activist and a minister but if you think about it that's what Jesus did. Jesus was always speaking up for people, speaking up when things were not right, and putting people in their place, when need be. Jesus and Martin Luther King Jr. used their voice, their gifts, their strengths, their weaknesses, their wisdom, and their faith to do what they were called to do.

Sister, I know it's hard sometimes to lead in the world we live in today. It's tiring to keep explaining why you deserve more pay, more respect, and have the choice to do what you chose with your body. Let me say this, God has called women to be leaders. A leader created us, in his own image. Our father is the head leader of this world. I am crazy enough to believe that His daughter is right under Him.

Sister, some days you might be afraid to speak up when things are going wrong. You might not think that your voice matters. You might think that you aren't qualified and educated enough to lead. There may be days when your past makes you feel like you don't have the right to say or do anything. All of those mind games and thoughts are lies straight and I mean straight from the devil. The enemy is doing his best to hold you hostage, because he knows when you become set free to be who God has called you to be, he's going to have a problem. Sister, the devil sees all your gifts and strengths aligned together that can be used in so many different capacities. That's a problem for him. Sister, you are a problem and, might I say, a good problem. A good problem created by the God of the universe that makes no mistakes. No weapon formed against you will prosper or interrupt the plans God has for your life. I feel like I'm in church today. If you're with me just say "Yes sis, I'm with you".

Can I ask you this, what type of leader are you going to rise up and become? The word says that you are a light. When do you plan to turn the light on? Are we waiting for a perfect time to lead? You have gifts and strengths that will lead people to break through. God has assigned people and things to you. Others don't have access to the things God has for you. Can He count on you to be a leader for those things He's assigned you to? Even if you don't have the credentials, the degree, the money, the team, or the platform. You can still operate in your spiritual gifts and be a leader. God is preparing things in the background just for you. You can't see them right now, but God just wants you to show up. To be willing to lead, to use your voice, to not give up, to be okay with messing up, to serve, to help create solutions, and to be a blessing to others.

Stepping into being a leader always costs you something. What are you willing to pay the price for? What are you willing to risk? Sister, you've always been a leader but now it's time to step into another level of leadership. This is your time to be a brave leader, a wise leader, a teachable leader, and a leader that continuously relies on God. You might be an organizational leader, an educational leader, a hospitality leader, an entrepreneurship leader, a healthcare leader, a financial leader, a social justice leader, or social services leader.

It's time to give birth to your spiritual gifts. You were given them for a reason. They weren't given to you by mistake. Birth them. Birth them. Birth them. Seek and find what your spiritual gift is from God.

Soul Food:

Take some time to talk and pray with God. Ask him specifically what your spiritual gift is. Let this verse assure you that you have been given a spiritual gift.

"A spiritual gift is given to each of us so we can help each other. To one person the Spirit gives the ability to give wise advice; to another the same Spirit gives a message of special knowledge. The same Spirit gives great faith to another, and to someone else the one Spirit gives the gift of healing. He gives one person the power to perform miracles, and another the ability to prophesy. He gives someone else the ability to discern whether a message is from the Spirit of God or from another spirit. Still, another person is given the ability to speak in unknown languages, while another is given the ability to interpret what is being said. It is the one and only Spirit who distributes all these gifts. He alone decides which gift each person should have". *1 Corinthians 12: 7-11(NLT)*

Soul Work:

Grab your journal sister. Do you know which area in your life God is calling you to lead? Ask God for direction. There are times in life when we might lose sight and ask ourselves what our strengths and purposes are. Don't feel ashamed. Take a moment and allow God to give you direction and insight. I also want to encourage you to find a leadership assessment or a strengths assessment to take. This may also give you more wisdom about your spiritual gifts.

DAY 20:

Financial Discernment

She seeks wisdom from God on how to properly steward her finances.

What thoughts come to your mind when you hear the words wealth, investing, saving, depositing, debit, net worth, equity, giving back, and financial freedom? Take a moment to pause and think. Before we go any further let's speak some affirmations over your life. Say these things with me:

- » I will be wealthy.
- » One day I will become debt free, in Jesus name.
- » My net worth will be larger than I can imagine.
- » The way I handle and spend money is going to change drastically.
- » I will have multiple streams of income.

- » I will be able to live the life I want and dream.

How did it feel to say those things? Saying big bold statements can be hard to believe but sister I want you to believe it. I want you to dream about it. I also want you to start working towards it.

Sister, I am not a money expert by any means, but there are wise people we can look to, who can help us change our money mindset. There are experts in the field that can help us learn ways to invest, spend wiser, and build wealth. I have added 12 questions that I want you to seriously think through one by one. You won't have all the answers and that's the purpose of the questions. These questions will get your brain flowing in the right direction. Some answers you will be able to answer and create action steps. For other questions, you may need insight from a financial advisor or someone that specializes in that area.

- » When can I set aside intentional time with God to talk with Him about my finances, and gain wisdom on the right approach to move forward in these areas?
- » How can I start paying off my debt, in small steps?
- » How can I have multiple streams of income that allow me to exercise my gifts and strengths?
- » What does homeownership look like for me? How can I end the renting cycle and walk into home ownership?
- » What services can I provide to generate income?
- » Is there a financial course that I can take to deepen my understanding of money?

- What are some books that I can read towards finances that can give me a healthier money mindset?
- How can I give more to charity, those in need, and wonderful causes with my funds?
- What are some ways that I can start investing the money I have saved?
- What will be my savings goal each month? This will help me with unexpected emergencies and open doors for other opportunities.
- Do I have to have the latest shoes, purses, and accessories if I have other financial responsibilities? Could I invest that money instead?
- What is a reasonable monthly budget for food, bills, emergencies, housing, and play money for the month?

Soul Food:

The book of Proverbs has so many gems of wisdom. This Bible verse is one of them. **Proverbs 10:4 (GNT)** "Being lazy will make you poor, but hard work will make you rich".

Soul Work:

Say this prayer with me, sister. Dear God, I have come to a place in my life where I want to change my financial habits. Please provide me with self discipline to save more, invest more, and give more. God, please send the right financial advisors to educate me in areas that I may be unfamiliar with. Teach me how to be a good steward of the money you give me regardless of the amount. Help me to break negative financial cycles in my family. I will become a better steward of finances. In Jesus' name, I pray, Amen.

DAY 21:

Doubt or Destiny

She knows destiny awaits her so she empties her soul of doubt, and fills her soul with thoughts of the impossible.

Destiny is defined "as your future or the pre-ordained path of your life". I know that destiny is sometimes hard to grasp because we are living in the present moment. We are living in the now. Sister, there is a destiny and a future that awaits you. It's already been preordained by God. It's already been established by God. He was privy to your destiny before you were born. Where you are now is not where you will always be.

I know some days it is hard because you are creating a life that you have never seen before. It might be hard to imagine because there might not be anyone in your family that is living the life you desire to live. I'm sure you have seen a glimpse or an idea of what you want your life to be like from social media or TV. Sister, be careful with admiring things from afar because that isn't the destiny God has for you. Things can look very beautiful on the outside of a home but inside could be a total disaster. Your destiny looks different from your neighbor's destiny. Your destiny looks different than your mama's destiny. Your destiny looks different than your family's destiny. Your destiny is only pre-ordained for you. You don't have to wiggle in your destiny because it only fits you. The size is you. Stop trying to shrink your destiny. Stop trying to match your destiny with something else. Your future is brighter than what your eyes can see.

I know you have been frustrated because each year looks almost the same. Trying to accomplish the same goals and then feeling defeated at the end of the year. Perhaps you thought you overcame something that keeps coming back. You thought you got rid of a habit but now it's become an addictive habit. All of this has made you believe that your life can't change. Your messiness has made you believe that you aren't worthy of a bigger destiny.

Sister, I told you at the beginning of this book that we were going to get to work. One of the things we have to work on is believing that we have an unbelievable destiny ahead of us. We have unimaginable things we are going to overcome. God has some opportunities that you are unqualified for in man's eyes, but in His eyes He has already qualified you because it is connected to your destiny. Don't doubt God. Don't doubt your future.

Here are some things that you can do as you await your destiny.

- » Get closer to God. Spend more time with God listening to Him and asking Him hard questions.
- » Once God answers your hard questions and prayers. Wherever He leads, just surrender and do what He says. Even if you have to do it afraid He will be proud and so will you.
- » Spend time in the word. A lot of the answers that we need are in God's word.
- » Live a purposeful life. Begin doing the things that make you happy and excite your soul.

Soul Food:

Take some time to meditate on these two scriptures. Write them in your journal or get a notecard and place them somewhere you can see them every day.

"It is the Lord who directs your life, for each step you take is ordained by God to bring you closer to your destiny. So much of your life, then, remains a mystery". **Proverbs 20:4 (TPT)**

> "Keep looking straight ahead, without turning aside".
> ***Proverbs 4:25 (CEV)***

Soul Work:

I want you to ask yourself two questions today. Take out your journal when you get a chance and write about these things.

- » What do you believe your destiny is? Take some time to study and reflect on the definition of the word "destiny."
- » What is God's destiny for your life? Sit in silence for a few minutes and just listen. See if you receive any direction or answers from God. You know God always answers our prayers so be open for answers as you go throughout your days.

DAY 22:

Confront Your Distractions

> *She releases her distractions because she knows she has a world to change*

Sister, I know some days you feel the weight of what you are capable of. You see yourself for what you are doing right now, but you know you are capable of something more. I want to confirm, that's the weight of your calling. That's the weight of your purpose. That's the weight of your destiny and your future knocking at your soul. That's why you keep feeling that weight, because the Holy Spirit is prompting you to change.

For something to change, something has to be disrupted. I'll say it this way, to spark change there has to be a tool, an intervention, or a replacement for the thing we are trying to change. I wonder if the change we need to make happen is connected to a distraction that has caused us to detour.

Sister, today I am calling us out to get us back on track. We have been detoured for long enough. Our distractions have taken enough of our time. Today is the day to confront the small thing so you can get to the big thing. Sister, can I ask you this - what is the "small thing" that you keep giving your focus to? What is the distraction that keeps making you go backward every time you try to move forward? Is it a relationship? Is it social media comparison? Is it negativity? What is it? Your future is bigger than this temporary distraction. The plans that God has for your life are bigger than the distraction that keeps coming in and out of your life.

Here's the problem: we keep avoiding our distractions instead of facing our distractions. We try to dodge them but they keep coming back.

Sister, God is taking us to a place that the distraction can't go. There is no room for it. Sister, I don't know what distraction you need to confront, but I dare you to confront it, face to face. I dare you to look that thing in the eye and say "You aren't welcome here anymore". Tell that distraction "I've got a mission that doesn't include you". "I got a world to change". "I got a generational curse to break".

Let's be honest. Mess is my distraction. All types of mess. Work mess, family mess, relationship mess. As soon as some mess comes into my life I shut down. My mind starts racing. I can't focus on the things I am supposed to be focusing on because I'm trying to resolve the mess. I had to have an honest wake-up call with myself. Foolishness and mess are always going to be taking place. I can't hide from it. I can't control some of it. But I can control the way I respond. I can control the way I make it a distraction instead of leaving it right where it needs to be. Now, don't get me wrong, if I need to address something I can take the time to do it but I can't allow it to consume me any longer. What is your distraction? By simply identifying your distraction, you take the first step to freeing your mind and soul.

Sister, I have to admit. I've wasted so much time being distracted by the mess. This book probably could have been written years ago if I had been more focused and aware of the constant distractions. See the enemy has studied our distractions, it's his career to get us off track. Have you noticed as soon as you start to get your life right and make changes for the better, a distraction comes? Bam, your ex messages you. Bam, some work drama starts. Bam, your kids start acting up. Bam, bam, bam, bam. Distractions just start flooding in.

Sister, we have work to do. We have a promotion to achieve. We have a therapy session we need to attend. We have some inner healing we need to begin. We have a book to write. We have a business to focus on. Don't allow these temporary distractions to become permanent distractions that deter you from the future and the life you hope for.

Even if you feel like you have wasted so much time being distracted by things. God will give you your time back. This book that you are reading today is a testimony of me claiming my time back. God can give you your time back. Deuteronomy 30:3 (MSG) is a reminder about time - "God, your God, will restore everything you lost; He'll have compassion on you; He'll come back and pick up the pieces from all the places where you were scattered".

Can we face our distractions together, sister? This isn't the day to beat ourselves up, this is the day to celebrate because we are facing our distractions. We are facing the thing that we have always tried to avoid but keep coming back up.

Can I remind you of this...

- » You are going places.
- » Our old stuff can't go to our new space. #ourdistractions
- » Our distractions take up precious time, which could be used to achieve His purposes for your life.
- » God can help us overcome our distractions. All we have to do is ask.
- » Confronting things isn't easy but it's worth it. #confrontyourdistraction

Soul Food:

Sister, I want to invite you to join me in going to a quiet space. A quiet space to hear from God. A quiet space to confront the distraction. A quiet space to hear from yourself. A quiet space to release.

Soul Work:

Today you are writing a letter to face your distractions. First, you will identify your distraction. Then, take time to write why it has been so hard for you to let this distraction go. Get to the core. After you have come to that realization, create boundaries and strategies of ways you won't welcome that distraction back in. Go easy on yourself sister. End the letter by asking God for His strength to help you overcome this distraction. We can't do this by ourselves, we need God's help in this area and He wants to help us.

DAY 23:

Social Mess

She begins to understand that God's algorithm is the best algorithm.

Sister, I hate to say this but I have to say it. Social media has become a social mess. Don't you miss the days when we could scroll through our app and just look at innocent pictures? I miss when we could just take pictures without pressure. Without waiting for the natural lighting. What was an angle back then? Now we have to take almost 50 pictures to get the right shot. I normally have to take about 100 photos because I'm looking for the right smile that doesn't show all the crookedness in my teeth. Then I have to make sure I'm standing on my "good side" so I'm not showing my extra weight". It's just gotten to be too much just to capture a picture.

Our minds have transformed to attending events not because we want to go, but because we want to capture the moment. We find ourselves spending more money on clothes, hair, and accessories. I believe that there are many great benefits to using the tool of social media. But social media can start to take over certain areas of our life.

One thing we're starting to see in group settings is less genuine interactions and conversations because of the attention to our electronic devices. Being in the moment is being traded for capturing the entire moment. We find ourselves being more distracted by our devices when we used to be more focused on details. As we scroll through various apps, we feel comparisons coming in, then guilt, and roots of jealousy start to unfold as we look through our timeline at the different pictures and videos. We begin to see our moods progressively change over time. Sister, I want to encourage you to unfollow people and accounts that don't make you feel well when you interact with their content. Follow more encouraging and inspirational accounts that lift your spirits and give you creative ideas.

However, it is a benefit for us to use social media and other tools that connect us to divine connections and divine opportunities. It is an impactful thing to be able to encourage people globally through social media. You never know how your content can inspire someone that's going through a dark season. You can shine a light on a solution to their problem. You can provide healthy services that can change the trajectory of someone's life. Sit with yourself and get to the core of why you end up on social media.

I often check my heart. I ask myself if I am posting for likes, comments, or new followers. If I ever answer yes, then I have to get to the root of that desire. I've learned the hard way that we as people will like you one day, comment and tell you're cute another day, and then follow you and be your friend the next. Then if a mistake comes or there is something the person doesn't like, all of that changes. You know how we are. Using social media isn't about the algorithm or the people, it's about you using your gifts to help people get closer to their destiny. Don't allow likes, new followers, or engagement to fuel your "why" on social media. I say this because things can change in moments. One day people will like your content and other days they will critique your content. Let everything you post or create be bigger than people's opinions.

Operate as a solution agent, a positive influencer, and a unique leader when you show up on social media. Be an ambassador for God on all platforms. It's okay if you don't have any brand deals because you're representing the best brand, which is God's kingdom. Nothing is more powerful than that. Sister, I know the algorithm is all over the place and you're shying away from showing up and promoting your services, but when you're doing it for God He changes the algorithm. God makes your name great and allows your gifts to shine. Not Instagram, Facebook, Tik Tok, or any of the others. Matter of fact, your name is already great. When people are introduced to your great name God gets all the glory because you're representing Him. Don't let a "little app" stop the way you operate and the way you show up. Keep posting encouraging messages. Share the tools with us even if you think we've heard it before. We've never heard it the way you deliver it. That's how we use social media and technology for His glory. When we add God to the social media strategy He gives us the strategy. Show up just as you are sister.

I also want to encourage you to take breaks from social media. Pick one day a week where you will log off for the day and tune out the noise. I try to do this one day a week, for 24 hours. I always see the benefits. Again, don't worry about the algorithm God's got that. Instagram, TikTok, and all the other apps aren't going to run our life. They can shut down permanently then what. They can make changes to the app each and every day then what. That's why your mental health is so important when using the apps. Sister, I'm tired of these apps manipulating us. Telling us when to post, how to post, and the way to post. Those strategies are wonderful but we aren't going to let those strategies shape the course of our day and life. We are no longer operating on their time and methods. Guard your mind and your heart while you are using these apps.

Another area I hope that we can be more intentional is when we are spending time with people we love. When we're at a dinner or brunch let's try and put our phones up so we can have quality time with the people we are with. I know we want to take pictures of our food (that's me sister), but let's get back to meaningful conversations and organic laughs. At family gatherings let's interact with our family and love them while we can. Let's cherish the moments we get to spend with them. Hide your phone if you need to, so you can spend some quality time with your family.

By no means am I bashing technology or all the wonderful social media apps we have. I believe they are huge benefits and they are helping the world progress. We just have to create and maintain healthy boundaries and self-control when we are using the apps. We can begin that today.

Soul Food:

Proverbs 4: 23 (NIV) "Above all else, guard your heart, for everything you do flows from it". This is such a great verse as we are guarding our hearts, setting boundaries, and creating new norms as we use social media and technology.

Soul Work:

Sister, I want you to create a challenge for yourself to take a social media fast.

First challenge: pick one day during the week that you will completely disconnect from social media. Make sure you do this for a full 24 hours.

Second Challenge: Pick a time when you will completely log off of social media for a week. You may decide that you need longer than a week, but pick a time frame that you can commit to. As you're doing both challenges replace the time that you would spend on social media listening to inspirational messages, doing things you love, connecting with God, and spending time in nature. Enjoy your break sister. I pray God transforms your mind and heart every time you tune out the noise. I also pray that the desires of your heart begin to flow from this choice, work, and obedience.

DAY 24:

Bible Intimidation

She has a new anthem, "Oh, the places I will go when I'm connected to the word of God".

    Growing up, there was nothing that intimidated me more than the Bible. I always felt like the Bible was this rule book that I had to follow. I felt like if I messed up in any area something bad was going to happen to me. For some reason, in Sunday school I didn't hear all the loving Bible verses and Bible promises. I heard all the Bible verses that focused on obedience, repentance, and sin. Those verses and stories are important too but since the emphasis was just on those things I tended to believe that the Bible was only made of rules. I would only hear about Noah's Ark and the 7 Days of Creation when vacation Bible school came around once a year.

That's where my love for devotional books came from. Devotional books felt more positive and more loving. They still included topics on obedience, sin, and repentance but it was spoken about gracefully. Devotional books helped me form my relationship with God. Sister, I'm sure you see now why I wrote this devotional book. Devotional books have shown me God's character and God's role in my life in such a different way. Each day I would be eager to read what the devotional reading was for the day. It was almost like a daily surprise. I love surprises so reading in that way made me feel like I was figuring out a mystery. All along I was learning who God has always intended to be, which is my father and my friend.

The biggest thing that God revealed to me through devotional books was His character. There are times when God is angry, happy, concerned, joyful, sad, and hopeful. I couldn't understand how God could operate in each of these emotions but that's what makes Him our father. A father that cares for us, a father that gets angry when injustice and bad things happen, a father that's hopeful for change, and a father that gets concerned by the behaviors we are displaying. I couldn't see how God could see and know everything and still love me the same. I didn't understand how God could love me and still bless me despite my abortion. He keeps proving to me that no matter what I do, His love for me remains the same. I've experienced friends who write each other off when something goes wrong. God's so different because when we ask for forgiveness He lets go of what we did. That's love truly forgetting my former ways and accepting me for the new person I am trying to be.

Understanding God's character has made me crave God's word. I've reached this level of curiosity about learning more about who God is and what He can do. When I entered the level of curiosity I started to trust God more because He kept revealing Himself more.. Before you can fully trust someone you have to trust their character. Am I lying sister? Trust begins when character is shown. Has God's character not shown in our life? Just take a moment and look around you. Start thinking about the trials you overcame. The blessings you received. The miracles you've witnessed and the growth you've experienced. That's all God.

As we are entering into a more intimate and deeper relationship with God we have to heighten our trust in Him. A deeper level of trust begins when we experience God's word for ourselves. Hearing God's word from our favorite preachers is good. Learning a different perspective about God from our family and friends is also good. However, getting to know God for ourselves is more intimate. You know if someone tries to set you up on a blind date and they keep telling you all the good things about the person and why it's going to work out. It's easy to think, "I've got to go and see for myself". You trust the person that's setting you up on the date, but it's not until you meet the person's character that you can begin to agree with those statements.

It's the same with God. You're hearing other people's perspective on God and that is helping your spiritual journey. It's now time to deepen your relationship with God. With time, the roots of a relationship deepen and also allow it to bear more fruit. That doesn't always mean the relationship will be peaches and cream. But even in the moments that are not so sweet, it's still worth it because there are areas of growth that will be learned through experience.

Sister, you might be like me where the Bible still intimidates you at times. I want to encourage you to pick your Bible back up. Maybe you need a different translation so you can understand God's word in a more receptive way. You might be a Bible scholar and you know all the verses, promises, and stories there are to tell. I'm encouraging you to go deeper in your reading and understanding of the word. This may be your first time opening a Bible and forming a relationship with God, take it with ease. Whichever category you're in I want to encourage you to get a Bible study book that takes you through the entire Bible over time. The Bible study book will be a guide for you as you are going through the pages of the Bible. It will have questions and insights to deepen your thinking.

Sister, there is so much that we still haven't learned from God. There's a story in the Bible that's an answer to your prayer right now. For the habit you're trying to break, there are specific strategies in the Bible to help you. If you've been questioning or wondering if abundance, the impossible, and God's favor is available to you, look at the many stories and promises that are found in the Bible. Satan wants to keep us feeling intimidated by the Word of God. God wants us to flee his intimidations so we can discover why we were created.

Don't stop listening to sermons, receiving wisdom from others, or going to church. That's not what today's devotion is about. Today's devotion is encouraging you to keep all of those things, but now strengthen your relationship with God in a different way than you ever have before. This starts by spending time in God's word even if it intimidates you. When there are times that you don't understand God's word while you are reading, pause and ask God for clarity. Write your questions down and give God time to answer on one of the pages in the good book. There's no better time than now to dive into your word as you walk in this new abundant season.

Soul Food:

This Bible verse gives me chills. I hope it has the same effect on you. "God keeps every promise He makes. He is like a shield for all who seek his protection". **Proverbs 30:5 (GNT)**

Soul Work:

Sister, as you are opening your word here are some sisters I want you to meet along the way. These are women in the Bible that have gone through similar situations like we have. There stories show us how to navigate through adverse situations. These stories are teachable moments for the world we live in today. Each of these stories has God's footprints, wisdom, and direction that we can carry with us each and every day. Here are some sisters I want you to meet.

- » Ruth - This story can be found in the book of Ruth
- » Sarah - Genesis 12:1-23 and Genesis 2
- » Rahab - Joshua 2: 1-24 and 6:20-25, Matthew 1:5, Hebrews 11:31, and James 2:25
- » Hannah - 1 Samuel 1:1-28
- » Abigail - 1 Samuel 25:2-42, 27:3, and 30:5, 2 Samuel 2:2 and 3:3 and 1 Chronicles 3:1
- » Miriam - Exodus 2:7-8 and 15:20-21, Numbers 12:1 and 20:1-16, 1 Chronicles 6:3, and Micah 6:4
- » Mary - Matthew 1:18-25, 2:23, 13:53-57, 27:55-61, and 28:1-10, Luke 1:26-80, 2:1-29, John 19: 24-27, and Acts 1:14
- » Martha - Luke 10:38-42 and John 11:1-44
- » The Samaritan Woman - John 4:1-42

DAY 25:

Welcome Aboard

She realizes there are 50 states, 7 continents, and 195 countries waiting to meet her.

    I remember at the age of 13 wanting to go on my first overseas, two-week mission trip to Panama. But this sister didn't have the money, the passport, or even the understanding about going out of the country. I was completely clueless. I remember having a conversation with my mother about how I needed to apply for a passport and how much the trip cost. Funds were tight during that time and all I remember my mom saying was "We gotta start fundraising, girl" with a huge smile on her face.

    Throughout the process of fundraising and applying for my passport there were so many people saying "Don't go" or "It's dangerous over there", and "Help people here". I remember thinking to myself. It's dangerous here in the US too. All the mass shootings and gun violence is dangerous. Then I realized the people that were telling me not to go were people that had never been on an airplane before and had never been out of the country. Always be careful who you take advice from. Sometimes the people giving the advice aren't qualified to give it because they have never experienced it before. I know they didn't mean any harm but they were just going off of what they heard, seen on the news, or learned through social media. If I had allowed those words to stop me from going on that mission trip I don't believe I would have the love for people and travel that I do today.

After that mission trip, I went on another to Brazil, in the Amazon, living on a boat for 2 weeks. I didn't have the money but God provided. Then I went to Kenya where I walked through communities that were marginalized and taught at an orphanage. Each country felt like home. I heard the craziest things about those places but they weren't true. I say all of this because it's time for you to see this world. It's time for you to see something different than your neighborhood or your town, your city, or your state.

God created this entire world for us to see. I promise you sister your home will be there when you return. The people that you love will be there. There's something about traveling that activates a side of your brain that you didn't know existed. Traveling has to become our new normal. After I got an itch for traveling I wanted to see more and experience more. I wanted to learn about other cultures. I wanted to meet new people.

Then God took me to Mexico, South Africa, Bali, Indonesia, England, and the United Arab Emirates, and the list goes on. Sister, Traveling is possible. You're hearing this from the girl that was brought up by a single mother that didn't have all the money. She just had a prayer and a fundraising spirit.

To all my sisters that are mothers, let your babies travel and see this world. Don't discourage them from seeing all the amazing things God has created. It will open their minds and introduce them to new possibilities and opportunities. I don't believe that I would have gone on half of these trips if I didn't have my mother's peace. I was so young. It was her peace that I carried with me as I boarded each plane.

Sister, you're probably wondering how I have been able to travel on a budget. When I tell you it's a tight budget over here, it's a tight one. Don't roll your eyes at me for what I'm about to say. I've been able to travel because I've said no to other things. Like getting my nails and hair done bi-weekly. The $40 I would spend to get my nails done, I would rather put aside to save for a trip. Now, trust me my nails still look cute and all I pay is $7. Look at the price difference sister. I don't have the latest shoes or purses. Instead, my joy is found when I wear Goodwill, Plato's Closet, and one of my sister's hand-me-downs. You will catch me here and there at the H & M clearance rack. I've learned how to make every dollar stretch further. Other than that I'm putting some money to the side for my next trip. Trust me it's hard to say no to some things but I rather have memories over materialistic things. Sister, I'm not over here looking crazy. I'm still able to look cute on a budget. I've just had to prioritize some things to experience others.

If you are one of my sisters that doesn't have to budget as much as I do, promise me that you'll make time to travel and go see the world. If you have it, go.

I also have to give a shoutout to my sister that has never ridden a plane before. Don't be ashamed at all. God's timing is always perfect. It doesn't matter what your age is, you can still get on the plane. Recently, I took two of my friends on their first plane ride, they are in their thirties. Now they don't want to drive anywhere, instead, they want to fly. They never thought they would be able to fly because of their fear of heights. God reversed that fear. Sister also please tell me how this makes sense, I am completely uncomfortable on rollercoasters and somewhat afraid of them but I love riding on airplanes. Tell me how that adds up. Airplanes give me peace. I generally go straight to sleep as soon as the airplane takes off. That's why I'm telling you to just try it. Say a prayer before take-off, chew some gum for your ears, and know that God is the ultimate pilot of that plane.

If you don't have a passport the time is now to get one. It's one of the best investments I've made in my life. I love how you don't have to get it renewed for 10 years. That means you have access to the entire world for 10 years for an investment of less than $150. If your passport needs to get renewed, take the time to do it, sister. Your eyes need to see something, your mind needs to be expanding to heights, and doors need to be open all around the globe for you.

How can you travel more? Here's what I would say in a nutshell. Limit some of your daily spending and put the money you would have spent to the side. Ask God to help you release the fear of heights and the uncertainty of experiencing a new place you have never been before. Ignore the wrong advice and see things for yourself. Invest in memories instead of materialistic things.

The place you have always dreamed of is ready to welcome you! Go see the world, sister, it's waiting for you! God will be with you every place you go. Imagine yourself in Santorini in Greece, Thailand, The Grand Canyon in Arizona, Niagara Falls in New York and Canada, Morocco, Maldives, Aruba, Mexico, Africa, Egypt, and Italy. Make your list of all the places you want to go.

Soul Food:

Sister, keep this Bible verse with you when you travel. "God will command his angels to protect you wherever you go". ***Psalm 91:11 (CEV)***

Soul Work:

» Take some time to dream and believe for a trip you want to go on one day. Decide to trust God for the provision to do above and beyond your budget.
» First, pick the place you want to go. It can be anywhere. Remember we are stepping into the impossible.

- » Next, research flight prices and the best months to travel to that destination. Look for accommodations, maybe a hotel, all-inclusive, or a resort.
- » Then, find the best things to do and experience when you travel to that place. While you're at it look up the best restaurants and food.
- » Lastly, let's budget for this trip. Take your calculator out and see how much you need to save to go on this trip. Look at areas where you can spend less so you can save more.
- » Remember to trust that while you can do all that you can do, God will do the rest.

DAY 26:

Trust the Transition

> *She stopped trying to answer her own prayers and trusted the transitions God placed in front of her.*

Have you ever felt the weight of your life starting to shift? Did this shift almost feel like a transition was about to happen? Maybe you couldn't put your finger on exactly what it was but you knew a transition was on the horizon. Whether it was a transition taking place at your job, a transition in relocating to a new area to live, or a transition in a relationship. All types of transitions have some type of discomfort connected to them. At times I would try and avoid transitions simply because I didn't want to experience change. I would resist it in every way that I could.

I wonder what would happen if we started trusting our transitions. I know that's hard because oftentimes we don't know what's on the other side of the transition so we don't trust it. What if we surrendered our plans and let God's plan take place?

Sister, let me tell you how I almost missed a blessing because I didn't want to trust God's transition. I decided once I finished undergraduate school, that I wanted to immediately go to Graduate School. I went to Graduate school to get my masters in social work. There came a time in the program when I had to apply to different agencies to receive my clinical hours. Sister, it was almost like applying for a full-time job. I would have to be there almost every day out of the week working and learning new skills in the field of social work. I ended up being accepted into an agency that served women and youth that had been sex trafficked.

I remember my first day like yesterday. I fell in love with what I was doing and I felt so inspired by the women I was working with. Every day my heart was tugged with a smile in so many different places. I was a part of the clinical team at the time so I was conducting individual therapy with some of the women in the program. Then I started teaching life skills classes. I never thought that I would enjoy the internship as much as I did. God is such a God of detail and intentionality. If I could have hit pause on my internship because time was moving so fast, I would have. It was only a one-year internship program, and time flew. Before I knew it, I was praying and asking God to lead me in the right direction as I transitioned out of my internship.

Sometimes you pray a prayer but then you decide you're going to answer your own prayer. Yes, that was me, sister. I prayed about the situation but then I wanted to direct God and show Him what to do next in my life. While I was trying to boss God around, I found an 11-month missionary program. It was amazing I would be able to go to 11 different countries in 11 months doing 11 different projects. One month I would have been in Thailand working at an orphanage, the next month I would have been in Africa being a teacher, then I would have traveled to India to be on the medical team, and the list went on. Isn't that amazing? I had made up my mind that this was going to be my next step.

Put a pin right there sister. Fast forward to weeks later my supervisor at my internship pulls me into her office and says "I want to talk with you". She then goes on to say "We really have been watching you this past year, and we are so impressed by all the work and impact you have made in less than a year". I smile and say "Thank you" but in my head, I'm like, "Get to it, go ahead and tell me what I did wrong". She then says "We want to create a position for you to join our team after your internship". I politely told her "Thank you so much for the offer but I am going to be a missionary right after the internship ends".

The next day comes and my supervisor asks to speak with me again. She starts to ask me what would make me stay in Georgia. I began to tell her that housing was one of the reasons why I wasn't staying in Georgia. At that time I was living with my family but I knew that wasn't long-term. My supervisor then said, "Let me make a few calls and I will get back to you". Before I left she prayed with me and we ended on "God's going to work everything out". I was driving home blasting my music on a Friday evening, ready for the weekend. My phone starts ringing. It's my boss again. Now sister, we just talked in person and we said we were going to "let God work it out". Why is she calling me again? I answered the phone and she said "Najma, I just got out of a meeting with our CEO and I told her your biggest barrier for not staying in Georgia was housing, she wanted to offer you a position at one of our other programs". "This position is at our tiny home community for women and children that have graduated from our program". "What if we gave you one of the homes"? "It would come fully furnished, it would be rent-free, and utilities free". "You would still be able to make your salary and have your benefits. Free housing would just be included". "Does this sound like something you would be interested in doing?"

Sister, my mouth just dropped. I was speechless. I didn't even have the words to say. "Hello Najma, can you hear me". My boss thought we had lost a phone connection but I was just sitting in awe basking in how God connected everything together. God showed up in less than 10 minutes. God knew I was fighting a transition that He wanted me to walk in. I felt God telling me "This is what I want you to do, this is the missionary field where I want you to serve, working with women that have been sex trafficked". I answered and said, "Yes, I will accept the position".

Sister, I get emotional when I think about this now. I didn't know at the time that a global pandemic was coming in a few months. The missionary program that I wanted to go on for 11 months got canceled during the pandemic and all the missionaries were displaced and had to come back home. See God saw things I couldn't see. God shielded me from something that I didn't even know was coming.

Sometimes what we think God wants us to do, is not what God wants us to do. Sister, imagine me being stuck in another country when the pandemic began. All I say now is thank you, God. When we put our trust in Him, God will do the impossible, beyond what we believe or think of. What transition do you need to trust God with right now? Don't be like me in trying to answer your own prayer. The transition may be uncomfortable and it probably isn't a part of "your plan" but trust God's guidance anyway. Surrender your plan and follow God's transition. Your transition is waiting for you.

Soul Food:

"God can do anything, you know—far more than you could ever imagine or guess or request in your wildest dreams! He does it not by pushing us around but by working within us, His Spirit deeply and gently within us". ***Ephesians 3:20 (MSG)***

Soul Work:

Sister, today we are going to get truthful with ourselves and God. Take out your journal when you get a chance. We are going to do some writing. Once you have your paper and pen, write down three areas in your life where you need to trust God more. After you finish identifying what those three areas are, pray over those areas. Then ask God to help you trust Him in each of the areas you identified. During this process be open to the transition that is about to take place in your life, sister.

Day 27:

The Power of Your Yes

She stopped and let go, she said yes,
and she let God do the rest.

Sister for so long we have given the power to the word "no". "No" I can't do that. "No", I will never change. "No" that isn't possible. I wonder what would happen if we transferred the power of our "no" to create power in our "yes".

I want to share a story with you about how God blessed my "yes".

I've always had this love for home decor, sweatshirts, t-shirts, a cute pair of earrings or jewelry, and stationery items like notebooks, journals, and planners. All of those things give me this joy and excitement. There's nothing like a fresh planner to write down my goals and dreams. Finding a cute pair of earrings to pop an outfit is always a win. The love for all of these things inspired me to open a Boutique for women. Here I was stepping into unknown territory. I have never sold merchandise before in my life. I contacted the Painted Tree (look them up if you want to sell items in-store) and applied to be a vendor. Here's the thing: when I was applying to become a vendor they were looking for vendors that had experience with online stores or had sold in stores before. I had neither. At that moment I knew I only had God. Fast forward, and I received an acceptance letter that I could become a vendor to open an in-store boutique. You see, when God has something for you it doesn't matter if you have the experience or not He will open the door for you and let you walk right in!

Sister, I want to show you how my "no" took over my "yes" when I started the process of opening the boutique. The store let me know in advance that we could not open until Summer because of logistics in the building. Which meant that I had more time to prepare. Then I delayed until the last minute, literally scrambling to get everything done. Have you ever been there?I had 5 months to prepare. Nervousness began to creep in and I started questioning God. I started questioning my decision. I started questioning if people would actually buy from the boutique.

Fast forward to the time of writing this book, when I paid 3 months of rent for an empty space because I procrastinated and grew afraid to move the products in. All because I allowed fear to enter into the mix. I bought products and was afraid to move them. Rent ain't cheap ya'll. I was comparing myself to others. I didn't think I could do it. I started wondering if I should do an online Boutique. Sister, it wasn't until the third payment came out of my account and I looked at myself and I said "Okay girl, something has to give".

I finally let my pride down and told God I was scared and nervous to go through with this project like I said I would. All I could say is "Lord, I need your strength". I started making a list of the things I wanted to sell in the boutique. One of the things I wanted to sell was inspirational sweatshirts and t-shirts to inspire women, but I didn't know how to make them. Companies were charging too much to get them printed. I prayed "God please help me learn how to make t-shirts and sweatshirts". I also added this in the prayer "God, I've spent a lot of money is there any way you can help me get it back"? I then set a date for a grand opening to invite family and friends to come and see the boutique. Another check off the list. After, I contacted contractors to help me design and create the booth. Finally, I took a leap of faith and started buying products for the store.

Sister, watch what happened when I surrendered and just said "yes" to God. The contractors that I reached out to told me that I didn't have to pay them anything to do the painting and building of the boutique space. My mouth dropped wondering how, why, is this real? They said "We just want to bless you." Then, one of my friends randomly asked how much my booth cost each month. Weeks later she gave me a card with the exact amount of money for the rent space. Another surprise from God. Remember I had asked God if He could help me get back the money I had lost. Remember the prayer I prayed asking God to show me how to make sweatshirts and t-shirts for the boutique? I went into Joann's Fabric to buy the materials for the t-shirts and sweatshirts and one of the employees volunteered to teach me how to use the devices to create them. I never thought that would be the way that God would answer that prayer.

Here is when God really showed off. Backtrack with me, sister. Remember when I set the date for the grand opening? On the day of the grand opening over 40 people came to purchase something and support me. While I was worried about whether people would come and shop I kept questioning if products would sell. Several products sold out. People came to the Grand Opening that I didn't even know! I kept wondering how I was going to attract clients and how I was going to get the word out about the store. Consistently now, things are selling at the store. And this is just the beginning!

I have learned from this that God wants our yes and He wants us to let Him do the rest. Throughout this story, you see how I was doubtful, scared, and procrastinated. It wasn't until I changed my mindset and gave power to my "yes" that I saw things begin to change. Your yes is connected to something bigger than you. Something bigger that your eyes can't see. I hope that my story encourages you to say yes to the very thing that God is leading you towards. I hope you learned from my mistakes. Invite God to help give power to your yes and then sit back and see what is next. Watch and see, great things are coming your way sister.

Soul Food:

Sister, take some time to read the story of Ruth in the Bible. You will see how Ruth's yes led her to something that she probably thought was impossible.

Soul Work:

Take some time to journal about an area in your life where you need to say yes to God. Ask God for help, guidance, and the courage so you can say yes to Him. Let this journal exercise be a place where you can be honest with yourself and God so you can birth your yes, which will lead you to your "next".

DAY 28:

Obedience Over Perfection

> *She knows that motivation will surely get her hands started, but discipline keeps her feet going.*

Sister, I have to say this. I don't like the words "disobedience or obedience" because they just feel like harsh words to me. They make me feel like I have to walk on eggshells as I go through life. Especially when they are used in a spiritual way. Every time someone mentions "obedience" I internally roll my eyes. Is that just me, sister? When church folks say you better be obedient to God or you know the consequences, that makes me feel like a failure. You probably can resonate with me on this. Obedience makes me feel like I have to be perfect. I think

I've felt that way because I've always put obedience and perfection in the same category.

Have you ever mixed two ingredients together that don't mix well? You realize that afterwards because the aftertaste is something you won't forget in your mouth. You might have blended two seasonings that don't taste well together at all. That's how it is when we try to put obedience and perfection into the same category, they don't blend well together. I love the Bible dictionary definition of obedience, it says "to hear God's Word and act accordingly". Why did I think that obedience meant acting accordingly in a perfect way? The definition of obedience doesn't state that at all. The word perfect on the other hand means "being entirely without fault or defect". They have two different meanings. Sister, we have to take a moment to undo these two words. If not we will be trying to live up to a standard that God never intended for us.

Obedience to God means, looks, and sounds like this: God, I don't know why you assigned me this task but I'm going to see it through. God, I accept that you are the only perfect person so I will rely on you to help me and show me your ways. God, please activate the Holy Spirit in my life. God, I love you so much that I want to be obedient to you but some days it's hard. I want to honor you but I feel like I keep falling short. I know I won't be perfect but I'm willing to become better. God, you told me to buy the house, apply for the job, start the restaurant, or end the relationship. I might not agree with what you told me to do, but I'm going to do it anyways. That's what obedience looks like sister. Obedience isn't about perfection, it's about change.

It's about surrendering and allowing a willing spirit to flow through you and give you insight into ways to become better. Obedience to God means having faith in God. This means there will be times when you don't know the outcome, but you're operating in obedience and trusting the person that provides the ultimate outcome. Obedience means we must sacrifice some things.

Sister, can we have an obedient girl season without the pressure of feeling like we have to be perfect? I know that God is taking us into new territory. I know that new territory requires a level of obedience. The obedient girl season means getting refocused on the main thing we are supposed to be focusing on. Do you get what I'm saying, sister? We might have gotten sidetracked from the main goals and top priorities. Let's get refocused. This obedient girl season means saving the coins for the vision and not spending the coins on foolishness. I'm talking to myself right now. Sister, I know you want certain things during this season, but the vision is more important. They will come in due time.

Here are 4 ways to have an Obedient Girl Season: The first way is: Organically reconnecting with God

Sister, we can sense when things feel phony and fake. You know we as women are super intelligent and our heavenly father is very intelligent as well. Maybe these past few weeks or months you lost your relationship with God because you might have been focused on other things. If that was the case this is a good time to reconnect with God organically. You could start journaling to God, having meaningful conversations with God, and giving things back to God. I am not sure if this is your first time connecting with God so maybe you can ask God to help you establish a relationship with Him.

The reason we have to reconnect with God organically is because God is about to reveal some organic and raw things to us. Things that we can not miss in this season. Instructions that He needs us to follow in this season. Places He needs us to go in this season. Ideas He is going to plant in our mind in this season. I said organic because we should want our relationship with God to be natural. Not filtered. That's a word right there. We don't have to go to God filtered, we can go to him organic. We can go to God unfiltered with all the pieces, all the emotions, and all the feelings that make up who we are.

The second way we can have an obedient girl season is: Turning Down the Noise

I believe that there are moments where we have to turn things down so we can take a moment to listen up. Listening up for the deposits that God is about to put inside of us. Take a look at your schedule and see what's working right now and what's not working. Are you feeling burnout? Are some people too noisy in your life right now? Turn them down sister, you have control of the volume in your life. Adjust any noise levels that are getting in the way of the most important voice that is trying to get through to you.

The third way to have an obedient girl season is: Structuring your Boundaries

During this season you might have to say no to some things. No, I can't go to brunch this weekend. No, I can't go on the trip. No, I can't go out tonight. When you set boundaries with people you are no longer trying to operate in obedience to them you are operating in obedience to God. Sister, I'm all about having a good time but we can have fun during this season with boundaries. There have to be moments where you say no to others so you can say yes to God. Think of some boundaries that have become loose over the past few weeks. Make some adjustments to those boundaries.

The fourth way to have an obedient girl season is: Shifting your mindset to Can

Sister, it is time to wholeheartedly believe that you can achieve your goals. Have you ever truly believed in yourself? What if you believed the impossible about yourself and expected the impossible to happen for you? All because you changed your "can't" into "can". It's time sister. Set a goal that you never believed you could accomplish. Keep speaking aloud that you can accomplish it, and get ready to see the unimaginable outcome take place.

One more thing sister, start this obedient girl season slowly. Don't try to be perfect in any area. Remember we are aiming for obedience, not perfection. This may be your first obedient girl season but this won't be your last.

Soul Food:

Sister, I pray that **Psalm 86:11 (GNT)** ministers to your soul in a way where you no longer operate in obedience like it is perfection. "Teach me, LORD, what you want me to do, and I will obey you faithfully; teach me to serve you with complete devotion".

Soul Work:

Sister, take out a blank sheet of paper and a pen. Then map out how you can begin having an obedient girl season. See how you can incorporate the 4 strategies mentioned above.

DAY 29:

Clarity Over Courage

> *She learned the way God solves problems always changes but God's faithfulness never changes.*

Sister, I know that we walk through seasons where we question what in the world is it that God wants us to do. We wait for signs, answers, clues, and clear instructions before we make a move. If we don't receive a moment of clarity we often remain stagnant. I've been in this place many times in my life where I just waited for signs of confirmation from God, people, or things. If I didn't receive confirmation I would just say "Maybe that wasn't for me" or "Maybe I shouldn't have been doing that". What if the confirmation was when God placed the vision in my mind? What if the constant nudging in my spirit was the clarity? There are going to be times in our life when we aren't going to know exactly what to do, when to do it, or how to do it. God just wants us to do it. Don't let waiting on moments of clarity and confirmation stop you from walking into your destiny.

Can we switch something up quickly? I know the culture we live in today shouts "Wait until you have confirmation" or "Wait until you have the sign". Now, don't get me wrong I love a good sign from God that says "Do it girl". However, I am setting myself up for unrealistic results if I believe that God is going to answer a prayer the same way every time. We serve a God of mystery and the impossible. We serve a God that switches things up and always keeps us wondering what's next. The way God solves problems always changes but God's faithfulness never changes.

Instead of waiting for clarity, I want to reintroduce you to courage. We know what the word courage means but sometimes we shy away from walking into it. Courage means "the ability to do something that frightens one". Sister, I know right now the very thing that you feel prompted to do is frightening you but I want you to step into it frightened. When you step into it frightened, courage meets you right at the door. Courage gets you to the next step that you would have never taken if you didn't go through with it.

Can I ask you this about the very thing that you are questioning? Is it aligned with your purpose? Is it going to bring a greater good? I know you're doing this because you love God, so I don't even have to ask that. Look at what Romans 8:28 (MSG) says: "That's why we can be so sure that every detail in our lives of love for God is worked into something good".

With that being said, if what you're doing is good you have God's approval that He's going to work it out for the good. Sister, you've been sitting on the bench for too long. Girl, it's time to get up. It's your time to get in the game. God is going to work all the details out for your good. When you take the first step God's going to take the next step, but you've got to take the first one. That's your confirmation. That's your clarity. Let Romans 8:28 always be your reminder when doubt creeps in to go for it. Take a deep breath, put on courage, and step into what God has been telling you to do.

Soul Food:

Sister, take a moment to meditate on **Romans 8:28**. Find a version that speaks to your soul. Memorize this verse and keep it at the forefront of your mind.

Soul Work:

You're getting off the bleachers and into the game today. What has been the very thing you are frightened to do that you know you need to do? What will courage look like for you as you step into a new level of your purpose?

DAY 30:

Overlooked

> *She is reminded that she never goes out of God's sight. She's at the forefront of God's mind. He sees her every moment, every second, every minute, and every hour of her life.*

There was a time period in my life when I was working for this wonderful company that I truly loved. The job almost didn't feel like work because I was so passionate about it. It wasn't until one day they asked me to help them select a candidate that would operate in a similar role like mine. The role was almost identical but I realized I had more responsibilities than the new role. It got to the end of the interview and they asked the potential candidate what their desired salary was. The candidate shared what her desired salary was and the administration team said "yes, that was the salary we were budgeting to give you". At that moment I felt overlooked, sister. I felt unseen. I felt used. I didn't feel valued. The salary was thousands of dollars more than what I was making. A significant difference. All the questions kept coming to my head. How was that fair? I have more responsibilities and I'm getting paid less. I have more qualifications, God, this can't be right.

I can recall another season in my life when I worked for a boss that I had more qualifications than she did. I had to train her in different areas but she was who the company chose to promote. Once again I felt overlooked. I didn't feel seen. I started to ask God "Am I doing something wrong". Why do things like this keep happening to me? I wasn't receiving any answers from God at the time but I kept feeling His peace. His peace was instructing me to be still.

I felt the stunt of my growth trying to be stopped at a season in my life. I wanted to try something new. I had outgrown what I was doing. My boss at the time would always make comments like "I don't know what we would ever do without you". "You fill so many shoes in this role". When I tried talking about moving up and operating in a different role she would give me all the reasons why it would be hectic and not a good transition for me. She kept reiterating how my transition would affect her. That's what you call people trying to build walls over top of you. That's what you call people trying to intentionally stunt your growth for their convenience. They love what you do for them but they can't see you operate somewhere else. Sister, don't allow those tactics to get in the way of what God has for you. It's easy to conform to something when roadblocks come. It's easier to say "I tried" and resume back to normal. No one is in charge of your destiny. No one can determine your future but God. People can try to manipulate your next steps but they won't get far because God doesn't play about you. He has plans for you that He isn't going to allow someone to interrupt. God is scratching all the agendas that people are creating and He is bringing His agenda to the surface.

God needs your help with this. He needs you to believe that when others overlook you He still sees you. God needs you to understand that every detour is only leading you to His destination for you. People don't have more power than God, He wants you to remember that. Being overlooked feels hurtful, uncomfortable, and doubtful. Sister, remain hopeful during this time. God sees your hard work and faithfulness when others don't. God sees the things you are doing behind the scenes that others don't see. God sees you as qualified. God sees you as the right person for the job. God sees what a financial increase can do for your life. God sees your tears.

Even though you can't see it, God is working. You're not being overlooked, you're being looked at by a powerful God. A God that has the final say. A God that can shake up the atmosphere so you can be where you need to be. A God that will fight the battle that you want to fight on your own. A God that says "When you see her know that's me, I don't play about what's mine". Sister, keep being faithful and do your part. Your seeds have already started sprouting. God has a different perspective. He is going to reveal what He sees at just the right time. What feels overlooked will be revealed as seen very soon. You are seen. You are heard. You are never forgotten.

Soul Food:

Psalm 3:5 (GNT) "Tears may flow in the night, but joy comes in the morning". It doesn't say which morning but we know one of the morning's joy will be there.

Soul Work:

Spend some time talking with God. Talk with Him about the ways you have felt overlooked and not understood. Let this be your time to release to God. Your form of communication can be in a prayer, writing in your journal, or simply having a conversation with God as you would have with someone else. Allow God to show how He has not overlooked you.

DAY 31:

She Can – She Is You

Dear Sister,

I wish you could see the tears streaming down my face. Tears of joy because you've worked so hard to get to this last day. I know some days you were tested, other days you felt like giving up, and you might have felt like the weight of the world was on your shoulders.

I also have tears of sadness because I hate endings. But, in fact, this is the beginning of living as the renewed woman you were always created to be. This isn't goodbye. This is actually hello, sister! Join me in saying hello to your new journey. Hello to the endless possibilities God has for your life. Hello to your healing. Hello to your financial freedom. Hello to the new healthy relationships that are coming your way. Hello to your renewed mind. Hello to your renewed relationship with God.

Say hello to your dreams and new ideas. Sister, say hello to the new you. I hope that you're proud of you.

Promise me that you're okay with messing up but you aren't okay with giving up. If you give up, radical change can't happen. Breakthroughs won't take place for some people because they are assigned to you. This is just the beginning of something new. You will be tested and you will be tried but perseverance is the only option. God needs your fingerprints all around this world. Everything that the devil twisted and turned for evil, God's doing a 360 and turning into your good.

She can... She is you... She can heal. She can excel. She can lead. She can succeed. She can start the business. She can get a new job. She can finish school. She can break cycles. She can finish what she started. She can write the book. She can go to therapy. She can have several streams of income. She can have multiple talents. She can make the devil mad. She is you.

Sister, this is your time. Your time to soar. Your wings are stronger now. Your wings have more muscle now. Your wings can take you higher now. Your wings can carry more weight now. You must allow your wings to fly. Go ahead and make your dreams a reality. Go ahead and start creating a life you've never seen before. You have to believe that. You have to keep believing more for yourself. Favor is coming your way. Abundance is at your door. Opportunities want to meet you where you are. Just keep pushing forward step by step. Every time the devil tries to distract you, tell him you're not the one! Your future is bright and he has no business there. Tell him he was able to lay hold of the old you but this is the new you. The new you isn't playing those games anymore. The new you dares the devil to even come your way because you now have weapons which are the word of God and the strength of God working through you. You're about to fulfill one of God's biggest assignments. Sister, don't shrink, and don't turn back. Introduce yourself to the new version of you. I'm standing on 2 Corinthians 5:17 (NIV) for you. "Therefore, if anyone is in Christ, the new creation has come: The old has gone, the new is here"!

Sister, the new version of you is here. Welcome to your new life. The old is now gone. God is doing a thing through and inside of you. Never forget this from Phililppians 4:13 (BSB) "I can do all things through Christ who gives me strength". Sister, it doesn't say you can do some things through Christ. It says you can do all things. She Can… She is you…

I love you, sister. You did it! I'm excited for your new chapter!

Your sister always,

Najma Calhoun

About the Book

Have you discovered the woman that you were created to be? Are you avoiding the calling over your life? Are there moments where you shy away from opportunities, talk yourself out of your dreams, and convince yourself that you can't do something? If you said "yes" to any of those things, this book is for you. Your perspective on life is about to completely transform over the next 31 Days. Your mindset is about to shift. God is calling you out and asking you to rise above your fears and comfort zone.

You're about to meet a version of yourself that you've never seen before. Your life will change because your mindset is about to change. You can get your joy back. You can release fears and finally stand on faith. You can let depression go and welcome peace. You're about to get more intimate with God. You've been hiding for far too long. There are assignments only you can complete. There's territory that you only have access to. I know the devil has been telling you that you can't do it, but God is saying that She Can do it.

About the Author

Najma is the Founder of the She Can Movement. This movement inspires women and girls globally to be who they are created to be, despite their past, their failures, and any life obstacles. Najma hosts the She Can Show which is a live motivational conversation packed with inspiration, encouragement, and tools to help women become the best version of themselves.

One of Najma's favorite things to do is travel and volunteer in missionary work. She started her journey on her first mission trip to Arizona to serve children and families on the Holbrook Indian Reservation.

Her travels have taken her to Mexico, Panama, Brazil, London, Kenya, Cape Town, South Africa, Dubai, and Bali. Najma was born in Buffalo, New York but raised in Tappahannock, Virginia. She attended Oakwood University and Clark Atlanta University and holds a Masters Degree in Social Work. For five years Najma worked with women that had been sex trafficked in Atlanta, Georgia. During the writing of this book Najma transitioned to becoming a flight attendant for a major United States Airline. In her spare time, she enjoys being with her family and friends, traveling to new places, journaling, spending time in nature, and eating all types of delicious foods!

www.ingramcontent.com/pod-product-compliance
Lightning Source LLC
Chambersburg PA
CBHW031631160426
43196CB00006B/367